A-level
Success

Sociology

AQA

Practice Test Papers

D1407244

Matthew Wilkin

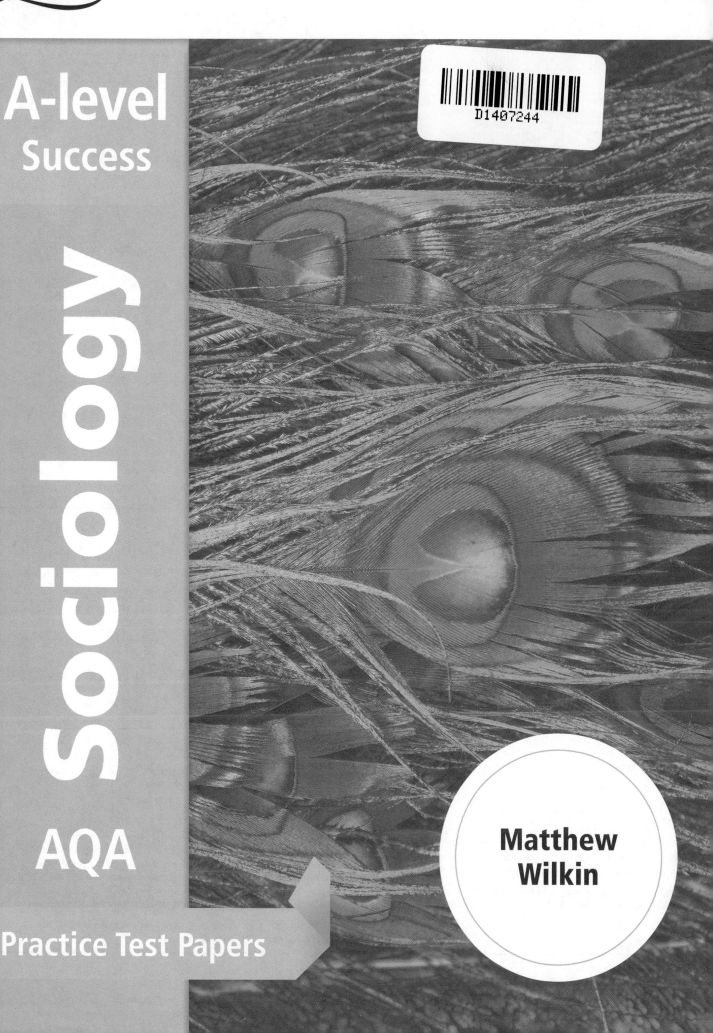

Contents

ACKNOWLEDGEMENTS

The author and publisher are grateful to the copyright holders for permission to use quoted materials and images.

Cover and P1: © Sutichak / Shutterstock.com

Every effort has been made to trace copyright holders and obtain their permission for the use of copyright material. The author and publisher will gladly receive information enabling them to rectify any error or omission in subsequent editions. All facts are correct at time of going to press.

Published by Letts Educational
An imprint of HarperCollins*Publishers*
1 London Bridge Street
London SE1 9GF

ISBN: 9780008179052

First published 2016

10 9 8 7 6 5 4 3 2 1

© HarperCollins*Publishers* Limited 2016

All rights reserved. No part of this publication may be reproduced, stored in a retrieval system, or transmitted, in any form or by any means, electronic, mechanical, photocopying, recording or otherwise, without the prior permission of Letts Educational.

British Library Cataloguing in Publication Data.
A CIP record of this book is available from the British Library.

Series Concept and Development: Emily Linnett and Katherine Wilkinson
Author: Matthew Wilkin
Commissioning and Series Editor: Katherine Wilkinson
Project Editor: Rachel Grocott
Peer Reviewer: Allan Kidd
Copy Editor: Louise Robb
Proofreader: Roda Morrison
Cover Design: Paul Oates
Inside Concept Design: Ian Wrigley
Text Design and Layout: Aptara®, inc.
Production: Lyndsey Rogers and Paul Harding
Printed in Great Britain by Martins the Printers

MIX
Paper from responsible sources
FSC™ C007454
www.fsc.org

FSC™ is a non-profit international organisation established to promote the responsible management of the world's forests. Products carrying the FSC label are independently certified to assure consumers that they come from forests that are managed to meet the social, economic and ecological needs of present and future generations, and other controlled sources.

Find out more about HarperCollins and the environment at **www.harpercollins.co.uk/green**

A-level
Sociology
Practice paper for AQA

Paper 1

Education with Theory and Methods   Time allowed: 2 hours

Materials
For this paper you will need:
Some paper or a notepad for your answers.

Instructions
- Use black ink or black ball-point pen.
- Answer **all** questions.
- Do all rough work on the paper or notepad. Cross through any work you do not want to be marked.

Information
- The marks for questions are shown in brackets.
- The maximum mark for this paper is 80.
- Questions carrying 10 marks or more should be answered in continuous prose. In these questions you will be marked on your ability to:
  - use good English
  - organise information clearly
  - use specialist vocabulary where appropriate.

Name: ....

0 1 Outline **two** ways in which cultural capital may benefit a student in their educational achievement.

[4 marks]

0 2 Outline **three** examples of patriarchy that may exist within schools.

[6 marks]

0 3 Read **Item A** below and answer the question that follows.

Item A

There is much debate in education as to whether mixed ability groups or streamed sets are the most beneficial to the pupil. For example, some subjects, such as maths, have tiered exams, so many would argue that classes based on varying degrees of ability are the most logical way to teach students in a comfortable environment.

Applying material from **Item A**, analyse **two** ways in which setting and streaming could impact educational performance.

[10 marks]

0 4 Read **Item B** below and answer the question that follows.

Item B

Statistics show that some ethnic minority students continue to underperform in education. Many sociologists believe that this is a result of factors outside of day-to-day school life.

For example, in many households young children have a large amount of responsibility around the home in the form of domestic labour and looking after siblings. This can have a serious impact on the amount of time that can be dedicated to school work and completing homework tasks.

Applying material from **Item B** and your knowledge, evaluate the view that some ethnic minority underperformance is a result of factors outside of the school environment.

[30 marks]

Read **Item C** below and answer the question that follows.

Item C

Investigating parents' attitudes towards homework

There are very contrasting views towards homework from parents of schoolchildren. Many parents feel that there is already enough stress and pressure on young children in education without the added weight of homework. Others, however, believe that homework is an essential part of education.

In order to understand the diversity of these views, sociologists may send out large numbers of postal questionnaires to parents, which allows for the collection of a range of views and opinions. This does, however, depend upon parents actually completing the questionnaire.

Applying material from **Item C** and your knowledge of research methods, evaluate the strengths and limitations of using postal questionnaires to investigate parents' attitudes towards homework.

[20 marks]

0 6 Outline and explain two arguments as to why interpretivist sociologists prefer the use of micro methods of research.

[10 marks]

END OF QUESTIONS

A-level
Sociology
Practice paper for AQA

Paper 2

Topics in Sociology   Time allowed: 2 hours

Materials

For this paper you must have:
Some paper or a notepad for your answers.

Instructions
- Use black ink or black ball-point pen.
- Answer **all** questions from **one** topic in Section A and **all** questions from **one** topic in Section B.
- Do all rough work on the paper or notepad. Cross through any work you do not want to be marked.

Information
- The marks for questions are shown in brackets.
- The maximum mark for this paper is 80.
- Questions should be answered in continuous prose. You will be marked on your ability to:
  - use good English
  - organise information clearly
  - use specialist vocabulary where appropriate.

Name:

Section A

Choose **one** topic and answer **all** the questions on that topic.

Topic A1 – Culture and Identity

0 1 Outline and explain **two** ways in which a person's sexuality may shape their identity.

[10 marks]

0 2 Read **Item A** below and answer the question that follows.

> ### Item A
>
> Many sociologists believe that although some of our gendered behaviour is natural, the vast majority is socialised into children by the parents. For example, the toys that are purchased for a child to play with are invariably gender specific rather than unisex, thus enhancing gender stereotypes.

Applying material from **Item A**, analyse **two** ways in which gender identity is learned during primary socialisation.

[10 marks]

0 3 Read **Item B** below and answer the question that follows.

> ### Item B
>
> Globalisation has had a huge impact on the sharing of services and products around the world. For example, the technology used for communication can often be found across the globe as a shared platform for interactivity.
>
> However, many societies are keen to keep their own traditions, cultures and patterns of behaviour that highlight their own unique identity.

Applying material from **Item B** and your knowledge, evaluate the view that 'many societies are losing their individual identities due to globalisation'.

[20 marks]

TURN OVER FOR THE NEXT TOPIC

Topic A2 – Families and Households

0 4 Outline and explain **two** policies that have changed the position of women within the family.

[10 marks]

0 5 Read **Item A** below and answer the question that follows.

Item A

The number of single-person households has doubled over the last 40 or so years; it is estimated that almost 30% of all households in the UK are now occupied by a single person. One reason for this could be the increased number of women filing for divorce since the 1970s.

Applying material from **Item A**, analyse **two** reasons as to why there are increasing numbers of single-person households in contemporary society.

[10 marks]

0 6 Read **Item B** below and answer the question that follows.

Item B

Post-modern sociologists analyse the changing nature of family structures and have noted a distinctive move away from the traditional nuclear family in many societies; the variety of family types is more diverse than ever before.

However, many theorists still believe that the nuclear family is the most efficient family unit in terms of provision for all its members.

Applying material from **Item B** and your knowledge, evaluate the view that 'the traditional nuclear family is disappearing in contemporary society'.

[20 marks]

Topic A3 – Health

0 7 Outline and explain **two** reasons as to why health and illness could be seen to be socially constructed.

[10 marks]

0 8 Read **Item A** below and answer the question that follows.

Item A

The health profession has increased its provision for mental illness significantly in the last 30 years, in terms of support and recognition for a range of different conditions, in an attempt to reduce social stigma. However, many forms of mental illness remain misrepresented, misinterpreted or misunderstood by large parts of society.

Applying material from **Item A**, analyse **two** reasons as to why there is often a negative stigma attached to mental illness.

[10 marks]

0 9 Read **Item B** below and answer the question that follows.

Item B

Census statistics show us that women live on average for around 5% longer than men do in developed countries such as the UK. This could be attributed to differing lifestyle choices.

However, many theorists are interested in the different ways in which men and women use the health service provisions they have access to.

Applying material from **Item B** and your knowledge, evaluate the view that 'health care and life chances differ for men and women'.

[20 marks]

TURN OVER FOR THE NEXT TOPIC

Topic A4 – Work, Poverty and Welfare

| 1 | 0 | Outline and explain **two** ways in which globalisation could impact upon unemployment levels.

[10 marks]

| 1 | 1 | Read **Item A** below and answer the question that follows.

> ### Item A
>
> Voluntary organisations are often referred to as the 'third sector' as they are neither public nor private organisations. The number of these aid groups continues to rise to support a range of different needs. Many sociologists feel that these groups offer a service that complements both the welfare system and the private sector.

Applying material from **Item A**, analyse **two** examples of provision that is supplied by voluntary aid groups to the most disadvantaged in society.

[10 marks]

| 1 | 2 | Read **Item B** below and answer the question that follows.

> ### Item B
>
> The overall aim of many governments around the world is to financially develop their country so that poverty rates can diminish and eventually be wiped out altogether. Scandinavian countries are often viewed as a model of how this can be achieved.
>
> However, neo-Marxists note that as a country becomes economically stable it simply causes the gap between rich and poor to become more polarised.

Applying material from **Item B** and your knowledge, evaluate the view that 'poverty rates decrease in a developing country'.

[20 marks]

Section B

Choose one topic and answer all the questions on that topic.

Topic B1 – Beliefs in Society

1 3   Outline and explain **two** reasons as to why religion may attract those from the lower social classes.

[10 marks]

1 4   Read **Item A** below and answer the question that follows.

Item A

One debate between science and religion is that science continues to progress and identify new ideas and theories while religion maintains stability and acts as a conservative force. Some sociologists believe this is a positive aspect of religion as it provides answers for its followers, while other perspectives, such as that of feminists, believe religion has become out of touch with the post-modern world.

Applying material from **Item A**, analyse **two** ways in which religion may act as a conservative force.

[10 marks]

1 5   Read **Item B** below and answer the question that follows.

Item B

The process of secularisation is evident in many parts of the world. In Europe, for example, the most recent census data shows a significant fall in those attending a place of worship or confirming a definite belief in a god or gods.

However, many theorists believe that using such data only identifies a change in the habits of religion rather than confirmation that secularisation is inevitable.

Applying material from **Item B** and your knowledge, evaluate the view that 'secularisation is an inevitable movement and process'.

[20 marks]

TURN OVER FOR THE NEXT TOPIC

Topic B2 – Global Development

1 6 Outline and explain **two** features of urbanisation.

[10 marks]

1 7 Read **Item A** below and answer the question that follows.

Item A

Many politicians identify education as the key to allow a healthy and developing society to breed a new workforce for the future. New Labour, for example, stated that the key to a successful society was for it to be structured around good education. However, Marxists argue that this requires an equality in the delivery of education for all.

Applying material from **Item A**, analyse **two** ways in which education can act as a tool for development.

[10 marks]

1 8 Read **Item B** below and answer the question that follows.

Item B

The provision of aid to less-developed countries can often bring more issues than first anticipated. For instance, aid can drive a dependency culture that can often prove more costly in the long term.

However, without aid many countries would be in a far worse situation than they currently are and would look to aid as an essential source of income.

Applying material from **Item B** and your knowledge, evaluate the view that 'aid can cause more harm than good in less-developed countries'.

[20 marks]

Topic B3 – The Media

1 9 Outline and explain **two** examples of news values.

[10 marks]

2 0 Read **Item A** below and answer the question that follows.

Item A

A study in 2011 showed that ethnic minorities appear in around 5% of UK TV adverts despite the fact that census figures from the same year show that the UK population of ethnic minorities is around 14%. Although poor representation of many ethnic groups has improved, there is still an issue in regard to the ownership and production of the media.

Applying material from **Item A**, analyse **two** reasons for the under-representation of some ethnic minorities in the media.

[10 marks]

2 1 Read **Item B** below and answer the question that follows.

Item B

Many sociologists believe that the events, lifestyles and behaviours of the middle and upper classes are over-represented in the media in comparison to the lower classes. For example, royalty often dominate the pages of some British newspapers.

However, the popularity of reality TV over the last decade has given rise to a far greater representation of the lives of the everyday person.

Applying material from **Item B** and your knowledge, evaluate the view that 'the media only represents the interests of the higher classes in society'.

[20 marks]

TURN OVER FOR THE NEXT TOPIC

Topic B4 – Stratification and Differentiation

2 2 Outline and explain **two** ways of defining a person's social class other than their occupation.

[10 marks]

2 3 Read **Item A** below and answer the question that follows.

Item A

Some post-modern sociologists believe that social mobility is far more achievable in contemporary society compared to the past, especially in relation to globalisation. However, others have noted that it is becoming increasingly difficult to actually measure the extent of social mobility, as the way in which social class is measured has become more complex than simply by salary.

Applying material from **Item A**, analyse **two** reasons why it is difficult to measure the extent of social mobility.

[10 marks]

2 4 Read **Item B** below and answer the question that follows.

Item B

Even in a multicultural society, ethnic minorities are still more likely to face issues of discrimination and inequality across a range of different fields, such as employment.

However, many sociologists point to evidence that shows this disadvantage is not only changing but in many cases, decreasing.

Applying material from **Item B** and your knowledge, evaluate the reasons why some ethnic minorities face disadvantages in society.

[20 marks]

END OF QUESTIONS

A-level
Sociology
Practice paper for AQA

Paper 3

Crime and Deviance with Theory and Methods

Time allowed: 2 hours

Materials
For this paper you will need:
Some paper or a notepad for your answers.

Instructions
- Use black ink or black ball-point pen.
- Answer **all** questions.
- Do all rough work on the paper or notepad. Cross through any work you do not want to be marked.

Information
- The marks for questions are shown in brackets.
- The maximum mark for this paper is 80.
- Questions carrying 10 marks or more should be answered in continuous prose. In these questions you will be marked on your ability to:
  - use good English
  - organise information clearly
  - use specialist vocabulary where appropriate.

Name: ....

0 1 Outline **two** ways in which people may be formally socially controlled.

[4 marks]

0 2 Outline **three** reasons why some ethnic minorities may have higher crime levels.

[6 marks]

0 3 Read **Item A** below and answer the question that follows.

Item A

Statistics show that the punishments for white-collar crimes are not as severe as the penalties for blue-collar crimes. Indeed, often white-collar crimes go unpunished altogether. This could be for a variety of reasons but one suggestion is that it is far more difficult to monitor and detect crimes of this nature.

Applying material from **Item A**, analyse **two** reasons as to why white-collar crime is often under punished compared to other crimes.

[10 marks]

0 4 Read **Item B** below and answer the question that follows.

Item B

Interactionists start from the idea that deviants are not characteristically different from others but rather that their behaviour is labelled as deviant or criminal by others in society. Therefore, interactionists believe that crime and deviance is relative in that it changes over time and from place to place as it is defined by each society and in each given situation.

Applying material from **Item B** and your knowledge, evaluate the usefulness of interactionist approaches to understanding crime and deviance.

[30 marks]

0 5 Outline and explain **two** disadvantages of covert observation in sociological research.

[10 marks]

Read **Item C** below and answer the question that follows.

Item C

Functionalist sociologists tend to focus on how a society works through understanding the connections between people and the agencies of socialisation; they aim to look at how people adapt to the environment in which they live.

However, other sociological perspectives have criticised the functionalist approach for focusing too heavily on the positives in society and ignoring the abundance of negative issues.

Applying material from **Item C** and your knowledge, evaluate the usefulness of functionalist approaches in understanding society.

[20 marks]

END OF QUESTIONS

Answers

Paper 1

0 1 **Two marks** for each of **two** appropriate factors clearly outlined or **one mark** for appropriate factors partially outlined, such as those outlined below.

- Elaborated language **[1 mark]** may be more in line with expectations of language by teachers and in exams **[+1 mark]**.

- Old boys' network **[1 mark]** – having contacts within education/governors may benefit the pupil, in university applications for example **[+1 mark]**.

- Hobbies/interests **[1 mark]** – having an interest in literature/an understanding of high culture/the arts may benefit language and understanding in education **[+1 mark]**.

- Mannerisms/behaviours **[1 mark]** may be seen as akin to the desires of the school.

Other relevant material should be credited.

No marks for **no** relevant points.

0 2 **Two marks** for each of **three** appropriate reasons clearly outlined or **one mark** for appropriate reasons partially outlined, such as those outlined below.

- Hierarchy **[1 mark]** – educational institutions often have more males in senior positions, for example, head teachers or university professors **[+1 mark]**.

- Focus of attention **[1 mark]** – teacher focus/time dedicated to male students may be more than to female students **[+1 mark]**.

- National curriculum **[1 mark]** may be androcentric especially in subjects such as history or business studies **[+1 mark]**.

- Masculinised language **[1 mark]** either used by teachers themselves or in textbooks/resources **[+1 mark]**.

- Textbooks/resources **[1 mark]** may contain stereotypical images of males in positions of power.

Other relevant material should be credited.

No marks for **no** relevant points.

0 3 **8–10** Answers in this band will show good knowledge and understanding of relevant material on two reasons showing the impact of streaming on educational performance.

There will be two developed applications of relevant material, for example interactionist views on labelling and the self-fulfilling prophecy theory, or Marxist views on working class students being placed into lower sets.

There will be appropriate analysis/evaluation, for example highlighting that streaming can have both a positive or negative impact on performance or relating streaming to social class and cultural capital.

4–7 Answers in this band will show a basic to reasonable knowledge and understanding of one or two reasons showing how streaming impacts performance.

There will be some successful application of relevant material, for example stating how streaming impacts the mindset or confidence of the individual student.

There will be some analysis/evaluation.

1–3 Answers in this band will show limited knowledge and understanding of the reasons for streaming impacting educational performance.

There will be limited application of material from the item, for example some general descriptions of what streaming is without linking it to performance. Some material may be at a tangent to the question.

There will be little or no analysis/evaluation.

0 No relevant points.

Indicative content

Answers may include the following and/or relevant points.

- Teacher labelling (interactionism) and favouritism towards certain sets.
- Self-confidence and self-fulfilling prophecy of the pupil.
- Sets may end up structured by social class (Marxism).
- Students may be motivated or limited/restricted by tiered papers.
- Positive impacts of streaming – increasing confidence and comfort.
- How materials and lessons can be appropriately structured to suit ability.
- Students may be motivated by the opportunity to move up a set.

Top band answer

Maximum mark out of 10

3 marks for AO1: Knowledge and understanding

4 marks for AO2: Interpretation and application

3 marks for AO3: Analysis and evaluation

Setting refers to how pupils are placed into ability groups for individual subjects whereas streaming refers to ability groups across all subjects. It is argued by sociologists such as Hallam that this style of education can both benefit and harm the educational performance of the student.

From a positive point of view, setting can allow for high ability students to push themselves to their maximum potential surrounded by students with similar ambitions and academic abilities. Keddie notes that teachers can often give students in top sets more creative work and privileges. This in turn allows students in the top streams to understand the nature and boundaries of knowledge, to understand expectations and encourages a thirst for knowledge. Many students in the top sets do not get held back by lower ability students. They become confident and the fact that they are labelled as gifted can lead to what Rosenthal and Jacobson call a positive self-fulfilling prophecy.

However, setting and streaming can also have a negative impact, especially for those in the lower ability groups. Power argues that many students in the bottom sets already see themselves as failures and adopt a fatalistic attitude to learning. This is particularly noticeable for pupils who are only entered for low tiered exams where a maximum grade has already been established. Lupton continues this argument by stating that students in lower bands often suffer low self-esteem and a crisis of confidence. It is also noted that once the label has been attached to a pupil, it becomes very difficult to move up a set or shake the negative attachment off.

Applying Becker's labelling theory we can see quite clearly that setting students by ability can have a significant impact on their attitude and behaviour in both positive and negative ways. The labelling theory has been criticised by positivist theorists and also by post-modernists for being rather outdated. It is also important to note that many schools prefer to adopt a mixed ability principle.

Marker's comments

AO1 – This gains up to **3** knowledge and understanding marks by outlining a clear definition of setting and streaming in the introduction and relevant terms such as self-fulfilling prophecy and fatalistic attitude in the essay. There is also good knowledge of key studies throughout.

AO2 – The answer gains up to **4** marks as it shows a clear interpretation of the question and applies a range of relevant theorists and studies such as Keddie, Rosenthal and Jacobson, Power and Lupton. There is also a clear application of the item.

AO3 – This gains up to **3** analysis marks by clearly looking at both the strengths and weaknesses of setting and streaming in equal measures. There is an evaluation of the labelling theory and the concluding paragraph offers an alternative to streaming in the form of mixed ability classes.

0 4 **25–30** Answers in this band will show sound, conceptually detailed knowledge of a range of relevant material on the factors at home that may impact the educational underperformance of some ethnic minority students. Sophisticated understanding of the question and of the presented material will be shown.

Appropriate material will be applied accurately and with sensitivity to the issues raised by the question.

Analysis and evaluation will be explicit and relevant. Evaluation will contrast the relative importance of both internal and external factors or the connection between them. Analysis will show clear explanation and appropriate conclusions will be drawn.

19–24 Answers in this band will show accurate, broad and/or deep but incomplete knowledge. Understanding of a number of significant aspects of the question; good understanding of the presented material.

Application of the material is largely explicitly relevant to the question, though some material may be inadequately focused.

Some limited explicit evaluation, for example considering to what extent home factors have an impact in comparison to school factors and/or some appropriate analysis, for example clear explanations of some of the presented material.

13–18 Answers in this band will show a largely accurate knowledge but limited range and depth, for example a broadly accurate, if basic, account of the reasons for ethnic minority underperformance. Understanding of some limited but significant aspects of the question; superficial understanding of the presented material.

Applying material (possibly in a list-like fashion) from the general topic area but with limited regard for its relevance to the issues raised by the question, or applying a narrow range of more relevant material.

Evaluation will be list-like/different theories will not be contrasted or one to two isolated stated points will be given. Analysis will be limited, with answers tending towards the descriptive.

7–12 Answers in this band will show limited undeveloped knowledge, for example two to three insubstantial points about ethnicity and education in general. Understanding shown of only very limited aspects of the question; simplistic understanding of the presented material.

Limited application of suitable material, and/or material often at a tangent to the demands of the question.

Very limited or no evaluation. Attempts at analysis, if any, are thin and disjointed.

1–6 Answers in this band will show very limited knowledge, for example one to two very basic points about ethnicity or education in general. Very little or no understanding of the question and of the presented material will be shown.

Significant errors, omissions, and/or lack of understanding in application of material.

No analysis or evaluation.

0 No relevant points.

Indicative content

Concepts and issues such as: family life and structure; single parenthood; home responsibilities; cultural and social capital; economic factors; language issues; parental expectations; fatalistic values; self-esteem. Writers such as Gilborn, Bourdieu, Bereiter and Engelmann, Evans, Lupton, Driver and Ballard,

Pilkington and Mac An Ghaill. Counterarguments can look at issues such as teacher labelling, ethnocentric curriculums, anti-school subcultures, and institutional racism.

Top band answer

Maximum mark out of 30

12 marks for AO1: Knowledge and understanding

9 marks for AO2: Interpretation and application

9 marks for AO3: Analysis and evaluation

Educational statistics show that some ethnic groups, such as Afro-Caribbean and Bangladeshi students, perform below the national averages at GCSE and A-level. Marxist sociologists believe that this is due to many external factors in the structure of society and the home lives of the students. However, interactionist researchers note that internal factors in school also have a significant impact on educational attainment.

As noted in Item B, the family life of pupils can impact educational progress. Evans identifies that many Afro-Caribbean families, for example, are single parent and therefore require a large amount of domestic responsibility on the part of the children. The New Right believe these families may also have more emotionally disruptive home lives, which also impacts upon the ability to study. Other more liberal theorists, however, disagree with this, believing that often single-parent families have a huge local network of support in the community.

Neo-Marxists also note than many ethnic minorities live in poverty and suffer material deprivation. This theory is backed up by the Swann report which explains that these groups are more likely to live in cramped or unhealthy conditions while lacking resources such as the Internet, textbooks or stationery. These conditions often impact the students' ability to complete homework or to carry out autonomous learning; skills that are often linked to high attainment.

Bourdieu's cultural capital theory is also relevant here. Often students are not gaining the behavioural attributes at home to take into the education system; this may include a fatalistic view of education or a non-conformist attitude. The students may also adopt what Bernstein calls restricted code language at home, which again does not fit in with school expectations.

This language barrier may also explain why some Bangladeshi and Pakistani students underperform if English is not used as their first language at home. Driver and Ballard found that those students who spoke their mother tongue at home often struggled with language and essay writing once in school. Likewise, Bereiter and Engelmann state how language is often a barrier for ethnic minority students.

Structurally, Marxists would also argue that society itself does not work in the interests of the proletariat, of which many ethnic minorities are a part. Althusser refers to this as the superstructure or ideological state apparatus, which seems to produce more opportunities for the white, middle class elite rather than serve the interests of equality.

However, interpretivist sociologists have preferred to look at what is actually happening inside the school environment to understand the underperformance of many ethnic minorities. Wright suggests that many schools are institutionally racist in that they continue to serve an ethnocentric curriculum focusing on the white, mainstream middle classes. Figueroa identifies that this is particularly noticeable in subjects such as English Literature and History.

Gilborn's research focused on the negative labelling of Afro-Caribbean boys in that they are often viewed by teachers to be challenging or less likely to accept authority. He suggested that this can lead to a self-fulfilling prophecy – the boys believed they would fail and therefore built a culture of resistance against the teachers and expectations of the school. This contrasts with the view that it is simply external factors that shape success in education; for interactionist sociologists, the learning environment and teacher/pupil relationship is just as critical.

This theory is further supported by the work of Sewell who argues that the educational performance of some black students is undermined by an anti-school peer pressure and an inability to take personal responsibility for this attitude. This again lends itself to a fatalistic attitude towards educational achievement.

Evidence of this anti-school attitude is reflected in statistics. Foster found that Afro-Caribbean boys are far more likely to be placed into the lower sets and streams and Hinsliff identified that Afro-Caribbean boys are also more likely to be suspended and ultimately excluded from schools compared to any other ethnic group.

Perhaps of most concern is that many ethnic minorities are still victims of racism. Aymer and Okitikpi identified that certain groups are still more likely to experience overt racism and report negative harassment and abuse from their peers – a factor which can seriously undermine educational progression.

Therefore, it appears that the underperformance of some ethnic minorities is realistically a combination of both internal and external factors and that actually the issues are often as a result of the social class of the pupil rather than their skin colour. It must also be noted that there has been a significant improvement for many ethnic groups over the last decade and a rejection of the negative stereotypes.

In fact, some recent government statistics now show that, while many ethnic minority groups continue to improve, it is the educational failure of white working class boys that is causing huge concern. As this latter group falls to the bottom of the educational league tables at GCSE level, we see how the fortunes of ethnic groups have shifted in the last decade.

Marker's comments

AO1 – This essay gains up to **12** knowledge and understanding marks as it clearly identifies which ethnic minorities are underperforming and uses neo-Marxism and interactionist theory. There is very strong knowledge shown throughout the essay of research studies and concepts such as the Swann report, fatalism, cultural capital, anti-school subcultures, superstructure, stereotyping and ethnocentrism. These terms are all relevant to the question and demonstrate clear knowledge of the topic.

AO2 – Up to **9** marks are gained as the interpretation of the question can be seen here through use and development of the item. There is then application of Marxist theory in the form of Bourdieu, Bernstein and Althusser as well as application of writers such as Wright, Gilborn, and Aymer and Okitikpi who specifically discuss the issue of ethnicity. There is further sensitive application to the question by showing how a factor may lead to underperformance.

AO3 – This essay gains up to **9** analysis marks through contrasting outside or external factors with internal school factors in a range of debates. Attention is paid to how both factors can contribute to educational performance. There are evaluative points throughout the essay and it considers how social class could actually be more defining than ethnicity. It also concludes by evaluating that white working class performance has now become a contrasting concern for many schools.

|0|5| **17–20** Answers in this band will show sound, conceptually detailed knowledge and good understanding of a range of relevant material on postal questionnaires.

Material will be applied accurately to the investigation of the specific issue of parental attitudes towards homework.

Evaluation of the usefulness of postal questionnaires will be explicit and relevant. Analysis will show clear explanation and may draw appropriate conclusions.

Students will apply knowledge of a range of relevant strengths and limitations of using postal questionnaires to research parental views on homework. These may include some of the following and/or other relevant concerns, though answers do not need to include all of these, even for full marks:

- Considers the practical and ethical issues of sending out questionnaires such as response rates, representativeness, generalisations, time and cost, as well as intruding questions.

- The validity of the research method: to what extent will parents be open and honest about their feelings towards homework?

- The sensitivity and ethics of asking questions without the child present: questions the subjectivity of the research and issues such as social desirability. The positivist approach to research may also be discussed.

13–16 Answers in this band will show accurate, broad and/or deep but incomplete knowledge of the strengths and limitations of postal questionnaires. Understands a number of significant aspects of the question; reasonable understanding of the presented material.

Application of knowledge will be broadly appropriate but will be applied in a more generalised or a more restricted way. For example:

- Applying the method to the study of education in general, not to the specifics of studying parental attitudes to homework; or

- Specific but underdeveloped application to the issue of homework, or discussing just the method rather than linking to the application.

There may be some limited explicit evaluation, for example of one or two features of postal questionnaires as a method, and/or some appropriate analysis, for example clear explanations of some of the features of postal questionnaires.

9–12 Answers in this band will show largely accurate knowledge but limited range and depth, including a broadly accurate, if basic, account of some of the strengths and limitations of postal questionnaires. Understands some limited aspects of the question; superficial understanding of the presented material.

Applying material (possibly in a list-like fashion) on postal questionnaires but with very limited or non-existent application to either attitudes towards homework or education in general.

Evaluation limited at most to briefly stated points. Analysis will be limited, with answers tending towards the descriptive.

5–8 Answers in this band will show limited, undeveloped knowledge, for example two to three insubstantial points about some aspects of postal questionnaires. Understands only limited aspects of the question; simplistic understanding of the presented material.

Limited application of suitable material, and/or material often at a tangent to the demands of the question, for example drifting into an unfocused comparison of different methods.

Very limited/no evaluation. Attempts at analysis, if any, are thin and disjointed.

1–4 Answers in this band will show very limited knowledge, for example one to two very insubstantial points about methods in general. Very little/no understanding of the question and the presented material.

Significant errors, omissions, and/or incoherence in application of material. Some material ineffectually recycled from the item, or some knowledge applied solely to the issue of homework in schools, with very little or no reference to postal questionnaires.

No analysis or evaluation.

0 No relevant points.

Indicative content

Strengths and weaknesses of postal questionnaires in relation to education and homework may include: time; spoiled papers; low response rate; poor representativeness; issues around the delivery of questionnaires; lack of consent from pupils; misinterpretation of questions; restrictions of closed questions; high reliability; questions around validity; quantitative data; subjectivity; social desirability; anonymity could increase validity and confidentiality.

Top band answer

Maximum mark out of 20

8 marks for AO1: Knowledge and understanding

8 marks for AO2: Interpretation and application

4 marks for AO3: Analysis and evaluation

As noted in Item C there are differing views among parents on the subject of homework and so a large-scale postal questionnaire could be implemented in order to track these views. Postal questionnaires are a primary research method that tend to focus on the collection of quantitative data. As a macro method of research they are more likely to be adopted by positivist sociologists.

There are many strengths to conducting this form of research. From a practical point of view questionnaires are fairly inexpensive to produce and schools will already have the sampling frame in the form of parental addresses on their school database. The questionnaires can also be sent out in an inexpensive way: in bulk or even hand delivered, as many pupils live near the school.

From an ethical point of view, the school can allow the parents to refuse to complete the questionnaires if they wish or to return them anonymously. Likewise parents can choose to not give their views on certain questions about homework should they find the question too intrusive. By allowing this anonymity the honesty and validity of the answers should also improve.

A key strength to this method is the size of the sample: if schools were to send out questionnaires to all parents then the results would be representative of the diversity of students on the roll. This in turn would allow the school to be able to make generalisations on attitudes in terms of whether parents are overall more positive or negative about homework.

The structure of the questions could include closed questions in order to obtain quantitative data with high reliability, meaning that the questions are consistent and repeatable and can easily be presented in pie charts and graphs. Some open, qualitative questions could also be asked to allow for parents to be more expressive on certain issues about homework, especially if they have particularly strong feelings on the issue.

However, it must also be noted that there are many limitations with this method. From a practical point of view the postal questionnaires can be a waste of paper and are not environmentally friendly. It would also take a little time to deliver the questionnaires compared to emailing them, which would be far more time efficient and economically viable.

The ethics may be called into question as there is no informed consent of the schoolchild. This could be classed as a sensitivity issue – asking for parental views on homework without the consultation of the student themselves. It could be argued that the views of the child are more valid than the parents as they are the ones who actually carry out the homework.

The researcher would also have to question the full extent of the validity of responses. For example, many parents may feel a pressure to answer positively about the school and issues surrounding homework; there may be a social desirability issue of parents answering in the manner they think the school wants to hear rather than how they actually feel.

Likewise, it would be difficult to quantify answers to the open ended questions as the reply will often be a purely subjective opinion on the issue of homework without a clearly defined viewpoint. There may also be an issue of the school cherry picking quotes from parents in order to suit their agenda, which could cause criticisms of bias, manipulation or massaging of data.

Finally, it should be noted that postal questionnaires have a low response rate and many parents are too busy to complete them or will simply throw such post away. This may result in only certain parents such as stay-at-home or middle class parents completing the questionnaire and therefore skewing the representativeness of the results.

Overall, although there are some benefits to this method, it would make more practical sense for a school to either send questionnaires out by email or to personally carry out interpretivist style in-depth interviews with both parents and children so that they can fully express their views on homework in an open and comfortable environment face-to-face.

Marker's comments

AO1 – This essay gains up to **8** knowledge and understanding marks as it looks at the postal questionnaires in terms of validity, reliability and representativeness. There is also strong knowledge of generalisations, response rates, informed consent, subjectivity and anonymity. The essay also has knowledge and understanding on all three areas of practical, ethical and theoretical considerations for the method of postal questionnaires.

AO2 – Up to **8** marks are gained for interpretation and application here because the answer does not just discuss the method; it links the method to the specific issue of parents and their attitudes to homework. The answer considers the issues of sending the questionnaires to the parents and potential issues in their reply. There is application of the item and links between the method and positivism and interpretivism. The answer maintains focus throughout by not drifting into a general methods essay.

AO3 – This essay gains up to **4** analysis and evaluation marks through having an equal balance between strengths and weaknesses of the method as well as considering positivism and interpretivism. The answer clearly considers the limitations of the method. There is a strong concluding paragraph that offers an alternative method to postal questionnaires and outlines the benefits that this would offer.

0 6 **8–10** Answers in this band will show very good knowledge and understanding of the interepretivist approach to research.

There will be two applications of relevant material, for example the benefits of in-depth research (verstehen) and the aim of gaining valid information.

There will be appropriate analysis, for example looking at the benefits of detailed and thorough research as opposed to gaining reliable/representative data.

4–7 Answers in this band will show a reasonable to good knowledge and understanding of the interpretivist approach to research.

There will be one or two applications of relevant material, for example some of the practical benefits of small-scale research compared to macro research.

There will be some basic analysis.

1–3 Answers in this band will show limited knowledge and little or no understanding of the question or the material.

There will be limited focus on the question, for example there may be some drift into a general discussion about methods rather than a focus on interepretivism.

There will be limited or no analysis.

0 No relevant points.

Indicative content

Answers may include the following and other relevant points.

- Weber's theory on verstehen and looking at human behaviour from 'in their shoes'.
- Symbolic interactionist views on gaining empathy and emotion from the individual.
- The benefits of validity in research compared to reliable/representative data.
- Examples of small-scale research in reference to observations, unstructured interviews, diaries, etc.
- The benefits of subjective meanings compared to objective facts.
- The benefits of empathetic methods compared to the scientific approach of positivism.

Top band answer

Maximum mark out of 10

5 marks for AO1: Knowledge and understanding

3 marks for AO2: Interpretation and application

2 marks for AO3: Analysis and evaluation

Interpretivist sociologists are also referred to as bottom-up sociologists or phenomenologists; they are more likely to study human behaviour on an individual micro level and so tend to opt for ethnographic methods of research such as observations or unstructured interviews.

One reason that interpretivists prefer micro methods is the desire to gain valid information. This means information that is accurate or trustworthy. Whereas positivists favour reliable and representative data, interpretivists favour a non-scientific approach to research. An unstructured interview, for example, allows the researcher to bond with the respondent, make them feel more comfortable and really express their views on a particular topic; an example being Hamid's study of young Pakistani females. By taking this approach the interviewer is likely to gain the trust of the interviewee, who in turn is likely to open up and provide honest and detailed answers to the questions being asked.

The second reason for the micro approach is what Weber refers to as verstehen, which means an empathetic understanding of human behaviour. Interpretivists believe it is important to see behaviour and attitudes from the point of view of the individual. For example, in Venkatesh's 'gang leader for a day' study he decided to actually spend one day with a small gang of drug dealers to truly understand the nature of their behaviour. This provided an empathetic understanding of why so many individuals ended up in their particular situations. For interpretivists, verstehen in research adds weight and depth to the research.

Therefore, interpretivists see many benefits to the micro approach, though positivists criticise the reliability of such research being repeated and also the low representativeness of using such a small sample to gain data. Positivists therefore claim that much of interpretivist research is purely subjective.

Marker's comments

AO1 – This gains up to **5** knowledge and understanding marks by showing a very clear understanding of interpretivist research throughout. Marks are gained for a clear definition in the introduction. There is sound knowledge of validity and verstehen as well as terms such as empathetic, ethnography and phenomenology used within the essay. There is also strong knowledge of studies to back up the two arguments.

AO2 – The answer gains up to **3** marks as it shows a clear interpretation of the question and applies a range of relevant theorists and studies such as those by Hamid, Weber and Venkatesh. There is also good interpretation of the question by applying the question of whether a non-scientific approach should be used for research or not.

AO3 – This gains up to **2** analysis marks in the overall concluding paragraph, making an analysis of the interpretivist approach by contrasting with the positivist approach and using positivism as a critical analysis of the interpretivist style of research.

Paper 2

Section A

Topic A1 – Culture and Identity

0 1 **8–10** Answers in this band will show very good knowledge and understanding of sexuality and the link to identity.

There will be two applications of relevant material, for example how sexuality can become the master status for an individual, and the way in which an individual may receive acceptance or discrimination as a result of their sexuality.

There will be appropriate analysis, for example expressing changing attitudes towards sexuality in many parts of the world.

4–7 Answers in this band will show a reasonable to good knowledge and understanding of sexuality and identity.

There will be one or two applications of relevant material, for example explaining the link between sexuality and masculinity/femininity.

There will be some basic analysis.

1–3 Answers in this band will show limited knowledge and understanding of the question or the material.

There will be limited focus on the question, for example there may be a drift into a discussion of gender rather than sexuality.

There will be limited or no analysis.

0 No relevant points.

Indicative content

Answers may include the following and/or relevant points.

- Master status – how sexuality can be key in defining a person.

- Labelling theory – interactionist ideas on identity and masculinity/femininity.

- I and the Me/looking-glass self theories applied to sexuality.

- Others' reactions to sexuality – in terms of increased acceptance or discrimination.

- Reference may be made to gay marriage laws in various parts of the world.

- Socialisation or nature/nurture may be applied to sexuality.

Top band answer

Maximum mark out of 10

5 marks for AO1: Knowledge and understanding

3 marks for AO2: Interpretation and application

2 marks for AO3: Analysis and evaluation

Sexuality refers to a person's sexual orientation or sexual desire such as being heterosexual, homosexual, bisexual or asexual. For many people their sexuality can be a key characteristic in shaping both their personal and social identity.

One reason why sexuality may shape identity is because it can become what interactionists refer to as a master status. This is the main or dominant status that overrides other identities. In this respect some people may overtly express their sexuality through their appearance, such as a homosexual male being openly camp or feminine in his dress, body language and communication. Goffman refers to this as the 'presentation of self' – that the individual is playing a role and transmitting messages and information to others with non-verbal communication.

The second reason that sexuality may shape an identity is because of the negative connotations some societies relate to gay males, lesbians or bisexual people. The New Right, for example, see homosexuality as evidence of a social and moral decline, while functionalists also feel it is a threat to the traditional nuclear family. These negative views could have a distinct impact on the way individuals see themselves. In fact, many homosexuals may even try to hide their sexuality if they feel they are breaking social conventions or norms.

However, it is important to note that attitudes to sexuality are changing, particularly in the western world, where gay marriage laws and celebrations of sexuality such as Pride are becoming increasingly popular. As Weeks states, attitudes to sexuality are social and historical constructs in that sexuality has a different meaning depending on the society and the time period.

Marker's comments

AO1 – This gains up to **5** knowledge and understanding marks by showing a very clear understanding of sexuality throughout. Marks are gained for a clear definition and examples in the introduction. There is sound knowledge of master status and negative connotations as well as key terms such as personal and social identity, presentation of self and social norms being used within the essay. There is also strong knowledge of studies/theory to back up the two arguments.

AO2 – The answer gains up to **3** marks as it shows a clear interpretation of the question and applies a range of relevant theorists and studies such as Goffman, Weeks, functionalism and New Right theory. There is also good interpretation of the question by focusing on sexuality and not drifting into masculinity and femininity or confusing sexuality with gender.

AO3 – This gains up to **2** analysis marks in the overall concluding paragraph, which makes an analysis of the changing views towards sexuality and that it is a term both socially constructed and ambiguous.

02 **8–10** Answers in this band will show good knowledge and understanding of relevant material in two examples of gender socialisation in primary socialisation.

There will be two developed applications of relevant material, for example canalisation/sex-role theory in relation to the language used by parents; the play and interaction from parents to children such as being more rough with the son and gentle with the daughter.

There will be appropriate analysis/evaluation, for example building on the idea from the item as to why most toys are not unisex but gender specific.

4–7 Answers in this band will show a basic to reasonable knowledge and understanding of one or two examples of how gender identity is learnt during primary socialisation.

There will be some successful application of material from the item, for example developing the idea of gendered toys in relation to stereotyped representation.

There will be some analysis/evaluation.

1–3 Answers in this band will show limited knowledge and understanding of one or two ways of gender and primary socialisation.

There will be limited focus on the question, for example some general discussion of gender or discussing gender in relation to secondary socialisation.

There will be little or no analysis.

0 No relevant points.

Indicative content

Answers may include the following and/or relevant points.

- Canalisation/manipulation/sex-role theory.
- Analysis of toys, colours and the interactivity of the toys.
- Verbal appellations/language used to each gender.
- Parental play and interactivity, for example being more physical with sons.
- Chivalry factor – parents may be more lenient or protective of daughter.
- Feminist ideas on priorities or attention being given to boys.
- Gendered names, colours, play room, books read to them, etc.

Top band answer

Maximum mark out of 10

3 marks for AO1: Knowledge and understanding

4 marks for AO2: Interpretation and application

3 marks for AO3: Analysis and evaluation

Gender refers to a society's perception of masculine and feminine behaviours and traits. This differs from sex, which refers to the biological differences between males and females. Sociologists are interested in the different ways in which sons and daughters are socialised by parents and they refer to this as sex-role theory.

One example of gendered socialisation is through canalisation. This means how parents channel different products and behaviours onto their children depending on whether they are male or female. As mentioned in Item A, toys are often gender specific, with action figures for boys and more maternal toys such as dolls for girls. Likewise, the colour of these toys are often packaged in stereotypical darker blues and blacks for boys and lighter pinks and yellows for girls. The way in which parents interact with the toys and their children is also noticeable; parents are likely to play rougher with their sons for example. Functionalists believe that the process of canalisation is how children learn norms and values in regard to gender specific behaviour, such as an understanding of the instrumental male role and expressive female role.

A second example of gendered socialisation takes place through verbal appellations. This means the way in which parents verbally interact with their children. For example, girls may be spoken to with a softer tone and referred to by caring terms and names such as princess or darling. Boys, however, may be called stronger names such as soldier or champ. Feminists believe that these verbal appellations are internalised by children and may explain why boys often take on positions of authority while girls remain more passive. They believe that gendered language is negative because it simply reinforces the idea of patriarchy.

However, there has been a growing trend in post-modern societies for parents to be less gender specific in their socialisation. For example, many toys and products now are unisex or a neutral colour; likewise, many children's books are trying to break away from the stereotypical gendered roles that we may have seen in the past. To a degree there has been a gender-quake in the socialisation of children, particularly in the western world.

Marker's comments

AO1 – This gains up to **3** knowledge and understanding marks by outlining a clear definition of gender in comparison to sex. There is strong knowledge of canalisation and verbal appellations as well as knowledge of functionalism and feminism.

AO2 – The answer gains up to **4** marks as it shows a clear interpretation of the question and applies two perspectives from functionalism and feminism to back up the points being made. The first point on canalisation also applies to and builds on the item. There is strong interpretation of the question throughout.

AO3 – This gains up to **3** analysis marks by clearly looking at gender socialisation from two angles: from a consensus/functionalist viewpoint and from a conflict/feminist viewpoint. The concluding paragraph also gains marks by evaluating how many aspects of gender socialisation are disappearing.

0 3 **17–20** Answers in this band will show sound, conceptually detailed knowledge of a range of relevant material on the significance of globalisation and its impact on societies. A sophisticated understanding of the question and of the presented material will be shown.

Appropriate material will be applied accurately and with sensitivity to the issues raised by the question.

Analysis and evaluation will be explicit and relevant. Evaluation will contrast the relative importance of both globalisation and maintaining individual identity. Analysis will show clear explanation and draw appropriate and relevant conclusions.

13–16 Answers in this band will show accurate, broad and/or deep but incomplete knowledge. Understanding of a number of significant aspects of the question will be shown, along with reasonable understanding of the presented material.

Application of the material is largely explicitly relevant to the question, though some material may be inadequately focused.

Some limited explicit evaluation and/or some appropriate analysis, for example considering how globalisation has increased and is continuing to impact upon more countries.

9–12 Answers in this band will show a largely accurate knowledge but limited range and depth, for example a broadly accurate, if basic, account of globalisation and its impact. Understanding will be shown of some limited but significant aspects of the question, with superficial understanding of the presented material.

Applying listed material from the general topic area but with limited regard for its relevance to the issues raised by the question, or applying a narrow range of more relevant material.

Evaluation will take the form of a comparison of competing positions or one or two isolated points about globalisation. Analysis will be limited, with answers tending towards the descriptive.

5–8 Answers in this band will show limited undeveloped knowledge, for example two to three insubstantial points about globalisation or identity in general. Understanding of only very limited aspects of the question; simplistic understanding of the presented material.

Limited application of suitable material, and/or material often at a tangent to the demands of the question.

Very limited or no evaluation. Attempts at analysis, if any, are thin and disjointed.

1–4 Answers in this band will show a very limited knowledge, for example one to two very basic points about globalisation in general. Very little or no understanding is shown of the question and of the presented material.

Significant errors, omissions, and/or omissions in application of material.

No analysis or evaluation.

0 No relevant points.

Indicative content

Concepts and issues such as: global development; Americanisation; language; homogenisation; multiculturalism; technological communication; post-modernism; mixed race/dual nationality families; geographical mobility/fluidity; secularisation; global events such as World Cup/Olympics. Writers such as Bauman, Lyotard, Baudrillard, Ritzer, Hall, Anderson, Strinati may be referenced. Counterarguments can look at issues such as functionalism, New Right, traditional values, national identity and the lack of globalisation of many LEDCs.

Top band answer

Maximum mark out of 20

8 marks for AO1: Knowledge and understanding

6 marks for AO2: Interpretation and application

6 marks for AO3: Analysis and evaluation

Globalisation refers to the process of integration and interchanging of world views, products, ideas and other aspects of culture. Examples include the spread of global products, language and international media. Some sociologists believe that this process is causing societies to lose their own identities; however, there is plenty of evidence to show that societies also maintain traditions.

New Right theorists such as Murray and Marsland believe in maintaining cultural traditions and therefore believe that globalisation is a threat to this. One example is brands and business: small, independent businesses are increasingly being closed due to the global super brand businesses in the world. For example, small coffee shops may suffer because of competition from big chains such as Starbucks, Costa and similar.

This means that small local chains disappear to global brands, resulting in individual identity being lost and replaced by products that are used by the masses in a variety of countries.

Likewise, supporters of traditional values like neo-functionalists believe that we are experiencing an Americanisation of culture. The vastness of American media is so powerful that it is having a hypodermic syringe effect on cultures outside of the USA: more people are dressing in American brands, digesting their media and adopting an American accent. It is noticeable that many people who speak English as a second language do so with an American twang, from copying American films and Hollywood culture.

Ritzer goes further with this debate by stating that many cultures are experiencing McDonaldisation. This means that the principles of the fast-food restaurant are coming to dominate more and more sectors of the world. He gives examples such as quick, fast-paced journalism, fast-track education and quick money-making businesses as trends that were first seen in America but now seem to be infiltrating many cultures around the world. Others have criticised Ritzer's theory by stating that it ignores the growth of small, independent businesses and those who are self employed.

Tomlinson believes that because of the global power held by countries such as the USA, this can lead to cultural imperialism. This means that their values become the dominant force and that their norms are considered more deserving than other cultures. According to New Right theorists, forcing one culture onto another is immoral and unethical as it assumes one culture is more important. Post-modernist theory often disagrees however, and states that many countries end up with a hybrid or fusion of cultures rather than simple imperialism.

Finally, the fear of globalisation for many theorists such as Dahl is that it leads to homogenisation. This is the belief that behaviours and characteristics become the same for everyone, rather than encouraging independence, uniqueness and cultural individuality.

However, many theorists such as pluralists believe that these fears are overstated. As mentioned in Item B, many societies keep their own traditions, cultures and patterns of behaviour and their own unique identity. Countries maintain, for example, their own language, flag, national anthem and traditional dress.

The pluralist Ang believes that globalisation has simply increased choice: many cultures do have opportunities to buy international clothing, brands and food but they also have the choice to buy their own cultural food too. Ang believes that customers have consumer power in that they make their own decisions on whether they want to buy global products or not. This can be criticised, however, as often small, independent brands are purchased by the major suppliers.

Post-modernists such as Baudrillard also note that globalisation has simply caused more diversity rather than cultures disappearing altogether; he states that people now have more choice, freedom and the ability to be geographically mobile. Therefore people do not always stick to just one culture but move in between and mix different cultures together. Strait continues this debate by saying that many individuals now choose and shape their own social identity rather than it being enforced upon them.

Hall refers to this as hybrid identities in that many people now fuse together different identities and styles rather than stick to one. For example, many people in the UK would refer to themselves as a British Muslim or black British; likewise in the USA terms such as African-American are used. In other words, culture has become less defined and more fragmented.

Lyotard therefore states that globalisation is not killing cultural traditions but rather mixing and matching cultures together. Two of the best examples of this are the popular dishes of chicken tikka masala and balti, which were created in the UK but obviously heavily influenced by the spices of India, Bangladesh and Pakistan.

Therefore, it is considered by many theorists that globalisation simply adapts cultures rather than losing traditions altogether. It must also be noted that while many places have been impacted by globalisation, there are many countries and societies in the world that are largely untouched by it, such as Inuits or

African tribes. Globalisation may have had an impact on the big, urban cities but for many rural societies, they continue to live a traditional way of life.

Marker's comments

AO1 – This essay gains up to **8** knowledge and understanding marks as it demonstrates a very strong understanding of the impacts of globalisation. The introduction defines globalisation well, with examples, and through the essay there is strong knowledge of theories such as New Right, functionalism, pluralism and post-modernism. Understanding is shown through key terms such as Americanisation, McDonaldisation, imperialism, homogenisation and hybrid identities.

AO2 – Up to **6** marks are gained for interpretation and application through the use of big name writers such as Murray, Ritzer and Baudrillard, and more contemporary writers like Ang and Dahl. There is strong interpretation of the question here by considering to what extent globalisation has had an impact and using appropriate material, theories and evidence to support the arguments, including application of the item.

AO3 – This essay gains up to **6** analysis marks through contrasting the positives and negatives of globalisation. There is also analysis, in questioning to what extent it has taken place. Evaluation marks are gained by looking at right-wing views on globalisation contrasted to liberal or post-modern views. There is a strong concluding paragraph that evaluates where the process of globalisation has and has not actually taken place.

Topic A2 – Families and Households

0 4 **8–10** Answers in this band will show very good knowledge and understanding of laws and policies that have had a direct impact on the position of the female in the family.

There will be two applications of relevant material, for example the Equal Pay Act, 1970 meant more females in employment; the introduction of the contraceptive pill in 1961 gave females more choice in when to have children and offered birth control.

There will be appropriate analysis, for example considering the increased empowerment the polices have had for women.

4–7 Answers in this band will show a reasonable to good knowledge and understanding of policies and their impact on women.

There will be one or two applications of relevant material, for example explaining the improvements of gender equality because of changes in laws.

There will be some basic analysis.

1–3 Answers in this band will show limited knowledge and understanding of the question or the material.

There will be limited focus on the question, for example there may be a drift into a discussion of gender equality in general rather than the impact of the policies.

There will be limited or no analysis.

0 No relevant points.

Indicative content

Answers may include the following and/or relevant points.

- Equal Pay Act, 1970.
- Contraceptive pill available on NHS, 1961.
- Sex Discrimination Act, 1975.
- Divorce Reform Act, 1969.
- Rape within marriage became a crime, 1991.
- Abortion acts (several of these in last 50 years).

Top band answer

Maximum mark out of 10

5 marks for AO1: Knowledge and understanding

3 marks for AO2: Interpretation and application

2 marks for AO3: Analysis and evaluation

A policy refers to the principles, regulations, laws or guidelines that are set by a particular government. In the last 50 years there have been numerous policy changes that have affected the position and role of women within the family.

One example of this is the Equal Pay Act, 1970 which determined that men and women should be paid the same for carrying out the same role or position of employment. Liberal feminists such as Oakley note that this caused a surge in the number of females going into full-time employment, causing many families to become dual income rather than simply relying on the hegemonic male breadwinner. This gave women more power and authority in decision-making and finances within the family. Dunscombe, however, believes that this simply resulted in the woman having to carry out the triple shift of paid, domestic and emotional labour.

A second policy that has had an impact is the Marital Rape Act, 1991. Prior to this law a wife was deemed to be the property of her husband and therefore in the eyes of the law he could not be seen to have forced, non-consensual sex with his wife. Radical feminists such as Dworkin campaigned hard for this law as they believe that females should rightfully be in control of their body and when they have sexual intercourse, not under the control and dictatorship of their husbands. Again this law shows an empowerment in the position of female rights in society.

Despite these policies, however, many feminists believe that patriarchy is still evident in the world today and more laws need to be introduced to address the unequal power balance between men and women. Although many third-wave feminists recognise the progress policies have made so far, particularly in the western world, they still feel we are some distance from achieving true gender equality.

Marker's comments

AO1 – This gains up to **5** knowledge and understanding marks by showing a very clear understanding of policies throughout. Marks are gained for a clear definition in the introduction. There is sound knowledge of the Equal Pay Act and Marital Rape Act as well as key terms such as hegemonic male, triple shift and empowerment used within the essay. There is also strong knowledge of studies/theory to back up the two arguments.

AO2 – The answer gains up to **3** marks as it shows a clear interpretation of the question and applies a range of feminism theories such as liberal, radical and third wave. There is also good interpretation of the question by looking at how the impact of the policy has affected the role and status of women.

AO3 – This gains up to **2** analysis marks in the overall concluding paragraph, which makes an analysis of the degree to which these policies have had an impact and ends with an evaluative point on where feminism and these policies have actually taken place.

0 5 **8–10** Answers in this band will show good knowledge and understanding of relevant material in two examples of reasons for increasing single-person households.

There will be two developed applications of material from the item, for example female financial independence/rise of feminism in terms of women choosing to be single; serial monogamy has increased with more fluid relationships rather than marriage.

There will be appropriate analysis/evaluation, for example applying the idea that monogamy is through choice in the post-modern era or that single-person households may only be a temporary situation.

4–7 Answers in this band will show a basic to reasonable knowledge and understanding of one or two examples of why single-person households have increased.

There will be some successful application of material from the item, for example developing the impact of divorce or fall in marriages.

There will be some analysis/evaluation.

1–3 Answers in this band will show limited knowledge and understanding of single-occupied housing.

There will be limited focus on the question, for example some general discussion about being widowed/death of spouse.

There will be little or no analysis.

0 No relevant points.

Indicative content

Answers may include the following and/or relevant points.

- Creative singledom and financial independence.
- Decreasing marriage rates.
- Secularisation.
- Rise of feminism/female independence.
- Rising divorce rates.
- More social acceptance of singlehood.
- More people going to university/concentrating on career/delaying marriage and children/longer life expectancy.

Top band answer

Maximum mark out of 10

3 marks for AO1: Knowledge and understanding

4 marks for AO2: Interpretation and application

3 marks for AO3: Analysis and evaluation

Single-person households are homes where just one person lives by themself. There are a number of reasons why single-person households have increased in the last 40 years. Some of the reasons for this rise are because of personal choice, whereas some of the reasons are circumstantial.

One reason for this trend is what post-modernists call creative singledom where an individual chooses to lead a single life rather than live in a monogamous relationship. This post-modern trend is on the increase and it is estimated that as many as 40% of all households in the UK are now occupied by single people. This move away from the traditional family structure can also be seen in the trend towards living-apart-together (LAT) whereby individuals do have long-term partners but they just do not reside in the same abode. Many argue, however, that these only make up a small percentage of households.

A second reason for the increase in single-occupancy households is as a direct result of the increasing divorce rate as stated in Item A. Since the early 1970s divorce rates have rapidly jumped up and therefore there is a tendency following the split for one partner to remain in the family home with the children while the other moves to a single residence. Rosenfeld identifies that two-thirds of all divorces are filed for by women and this often results in the man moving away from the family home and into a single-person residence, and the woman living with the children. The result of this is more multi-generational families, in which each generation has one or very few members – these are known as beanpole families. However, it can be argued that the divorce rate has fallen in the last decade in the UK.

It must be noted, however, that often single-person households are simply a transitional phase. For example, many young people live as a single person before they meet a partner and many divorced people live as a single person before forming new, reconstituted families. Therefore many single households are simply transitional households as opposed to a permanent state of residence.

Marker's comments

AO1 – This gains up to **3** knowledge and understanding marks by outlining a clear definition of single-person households. There is strong knowledge of creative singledom and divorce as well as knowledge of monogamy, LATs and beanpole families.

AO2 – The answer gains up to **4** marks as it shows a clear interpretation of the question and applies two very different reasons for single living. The first point on creative singledom applies lots of key terms and language while the second point on divorce applies and builds on the item and use of the writer Rosenfeld. There is strong interpretation of the question throughout.

AO3 – This gains up to **3** analysis marks by clearly looking at single households from two angles: from a personal choice point of view and then from an enforced viewpoint. The concluding paragraph also gains marks by evaluating how living as a single person is often a transitional rather than permanent state.

0 6 **17–20** Answers in this band will show sound, conceptually detailed knowledge of a range of relevant material on the reduction of the traditional nuclear family. A sophisticated understanding of the question and of the presented material will be shown.

Appropriate material will be applied accurately and with sensitivity to the issues raised by the question.

Analysis and evaluation will be explicit and relevant. Evaluation may be developed, for instance by contrasting post-modernism to more traditional views such as functionalism and the New Right. Analysis will show clear explanation and draw appropriate and relevant conclusions.

13–16 Answers in this band will show accurate, broad and/or deep but incomplete knowledge. There will be understanding of a number of significant aspects of the question as well as reasonable understanding of the presented material.

Application of the material is largely explicitly relevant to the question, though some material may be inadequately focused.

Some limited explicit evaluation and analysis, for example a debate about where the nuclear family is decreasing compared to where it remains common.

9–12 Answers in this band will show a largely accurate knowledge but limited range and depth, for example a basic account of different types of families other than the nuclear family. Understands some limited but significant aspects of the question; superficial understanding of the presented material.

Applying listed material from the general topic area but with limited regard for its relevance to the issues raised by the question, or applying a narrow range of more relevant material.

Evaluation will take the form of a comparison of competing positions or one or two isolated points about globalisation. Analysis will be limited, with answers tending towards the descriptive.

5–8 Answers in this band will show limited undeveloped knowledge, for example two to three insubstantial points about the nuclear family or post-modernism in general. Understanding will be of only very limited aspects of the question, with simplistic understanding of the presented material.

Limited application of suitable material, and/or material often at a tangent to the demands of the question.

Very limited or no evaluation. Attempts at analysis, if any, are thin and disjointed.

1–4 Answers in this band will show a very limited knowledge, for example one to two very basic points about family changes or simply defining the nuclear family. Very little or no understanding of the question and of the presented material.

Significant errors, omissions, and/or omissions in application of material.

No analysis or evaluation.

0 No relevant points.

Indicative content

Concepts and issues such as: globalisation; secularisation; geographical mobility; increased singledom; rising divorce rates; falling marriage rates; childless couples; serial monogamy; gay marriage; cohabitation; blended/reconstituted families; more policies and help for single-parent families; changes in social attitudes; impacts of feminism; higher expectations of relationships; financial independence. Counterarguments from functionalism, the New Right and also societies that still maintain the traditional nuclear family. Writers such as Giddens, Chester, and Rappoport and Rappoport may be applied.

Top band answer

Maximum mark out of 20

8 marks for AO1: Knowledge and understanding

6 marks for AO2: Interpretation and application

6 marks for AO3: Analysis and evaluation

A nuclear family refers to the traditional unit of a couple and their offspring. The functionalist Murdock elaborates by saying a family includes adults of both sexes, at least two of whom maintain a socially approved sexual relationship, and one or more children. Post-modernists believe that this type of family is disappearing, though more traditional theorists feel there is still plenty of evidence for the existence of the nuclear family.

Post-modernists such as Bauman and Lyotard note how contemporary family structures are now far more diverse than they used to be. Single-parent, reconstituted, single-sex, cohabiting and beanpole families are all on the increase as the traditional nuclear family decreases in popularity. There are numerous social reasons for this adaptation.

Statistical evidence on the reduction of nuclear families can be seen in both marriage and divorce rates: the number of people marrying has fallen in recent times and in 2001 the lowest number of marriages took place in the UK since records began. Conversely, divorce rates have steadily increased with around 40% of all marriages ending in divorce. Both of these trends result in more single-person households, cohabiting couples or beanpole families. However, it should be noted that divorce rates have reduced in the last decade and marriage rates continue to fluctuate.

Likewise, more couples are now choosing to not have children. Plummer noted the number of childless women at the age of 45 has more than doubled in the last 40 years, noting that cost and lack of free time are common reasons for remaining childless. There has also been an increase in what feminists refer to as alpha females: those that wish to dedicate time and attention to a career rather than motherhood. It should be noted, however, that these are not trends found across all parts of the world.

Weeks and Donovan outline that there has also been an increase in single-sex couples. This is due to a combination of a change in attitudes, increased acceptance, secularisation and in particular a change in laws allowing gay people to marry. In 2016, 20 countries around the world now allow people of the same sex to marry, a number which looks set to increase even more in the near future, though of course this is still illegal in many cultures.

Finally, more people are also choosing what post-modernists refer to as creative singledom. This is when an individual makes the life choice to be single. Many theorists have noted that financially it is far more beneficial to only be responsible for yourself, allowing for more disposable income for travel and materialism, as well as a sense of freedom. This choice may also allow the individual to explore multiple partners, promiscuity or serial monogamy rather than living with a long-term partner. Rappoport and Rappoport often refer to these changes when discussing the vast increase of family diversities.

Despite all these changes, more traditional perspectives such as functionalism and New Right theorists believe that the nuclear family still has an important role to play in society. Murray notes for instance that although nuclear families are decreasing, they are still the most common type of family and indeed in 2002, 78% of all UK children lived in a nuclear family.

Neo-functionalists also argue that most people still desire to live in a nuclear family at some point in their lives. For example, many couples that are cohabiting will one day become a nuclear family but they are simply delaying the time at which they will get married or have children. Statistics collated from researchers such as Chester support this view in that the average age of marriage and first time parenthood now comes much later on in life.

Likewise, the desire to be in a nuclear family can be evidenced in the increasing number of reconstituted families, also known as step or blended families. This shows that although many families go through divorce, this is often short lived or a transient stage before starting a new family once again. There is more social acceptance of this than before; Weeks refers to this as the increased choice in morality.

The post-modernist Beck suggests that what is occurring in contemporary society is an increase in the negotiated family. By this he means that family units are simply varying according to the changing needs of the people in them. Beck states that although nuclear families are less stable than they used to be, people tend to drift in and out of them rather than maintain a long-term, permanent state.

Therefore, it is very difficult to identify if the nuclear family is truly disappearing or not. If we were to take Murdock's definition of a family then perhaps it would be fair to say this type of family has decreased. However, the nuclear family does still exist but in slightly different forms than before, such as the reconstituted family or the single-sex family with adopted children.

What is important to note, however, is that this pattern of diversity may be true in countries such as the UK, but in many parts of the world the traditional nuclear family is still very much a bedrock of society. It is most noticeable in countries with a strong religious grounding. Indeed, across the world the nuclear family is still the most common and popular family type, far beyond all other options.

Marker's comments

AO1 – This essay gains up to **8** knowledge and understanding marks as it demonstrates a very strong understanding of the nuclear family and how it has changed. The introduction defines the nuclear family well before applying functionalism/neo-functionalism and post-modern theory throughout as well as backing up points with statistics. Understanding is shown through key terms such as cohabitation, alpha female, secularisation, creative singledom, reconstituted and negotiated families.

AO2 – Up to **6** marks are gained for interpretation and application through building on the post-modern theory as stated in the item. The material, theories and evidence to support the argument can be seen through the application of Bauman, Plummer, Weeks and Donovan and in counterarguments through the application of Murray and Beck. There has been very good interpretation and selection of relevant writers throughout.

AO3 – This essay gains up to **6** analysis marks through contrasting evidence for and against the view that the nuclear family is disappearing. There is also analysis in comparing traditional views such as functionalism with contemporary theory in post-modernism. Evaluation marks are gained by looking at how the family is changing and being delayed rather than disappearing altogether. There is also evaluative marks in the final paragraph gained through stating that family structures differ between societies.

Topic A3 – Health

0 7 **8–10** Answers in this band will show very good knowledge and understanding of the social construction of health and illness.

There will be two applications of relevant material, for example the difference in stigmatisation of health from society to society and that many illnesses are contested or questioned, such as chronic fatigue or even ADHD.

There will be appropriate analysis, for example considering that the number of illnesses, allergies and conditions increases over time.

4–7 Answers in this band will show a reasonable to good knowledge and understanding of how illnesses could be socially constructed.

There will be one or two applications of relevant material, for example discussing how the definition of a condition differs from society to society.

There will be some basic analysis.

1–3 Answers in this band will show limited knowledge and understanding of the question or the material.

There will be limited focus on the question, for example there may be a drift into a general discussion of health and illness unrelated to the idea of social construction.

There will be limited or no analysis.

0 No relevant points.

Indicative content

Answers may include the following and/or relevant points.

- Stigmatisation of health and conditions.
- Contested illnesses and allergies.
- Perception of health and illnesses in different societies.
- The changes in defining or understanding an illness over time.
- The subjectivity of pain levels.
- Medical companies generating concerns to increase sales.
- The difficulty of defining mental illness.

Top band answer

Maximum mark out of 10

5 marks for AO1: Knowledge and understanding

3 marks for AO2: Interpretation and application

2 marks for AO3: Analysis and evaluation

The term socially constructed means something that is created and developed by society or through cultural and social practice rather than something that is biologically natural. Many sociologists believe that elements of health and illness are determined by society rather than a natural illness.

The first example of this can be seen through the 'social model' theory that believes environmental, social and behavioural factors all contribute to make a person ill. A simple analysis of a condition such as a chest infection or even pneumonia can be related to the environment a person lives in. For example, a home with dampness or a heavily polluted city would contribute to the ill health of the individual. Marxists back up this viewpoint by using statistics to show the poor have a much lower life expectancy than those from the ruling classes. Access to clean water and sanitation are two clear markers and contributions to the levels of health.

A second example of the social construction of health can be identified in how different societies label and treat ill health. Senior and Viveash note that some conditions such as chronic fatigue or ADHD would not be recognised in certain parts of the world; each country would define these conditions slightly differently. In some societies people are far more likely to visit the doctor and be diagnosed and treated for a condition while in other societies this would go largely untreated. The sociologist Last refers to this as the clinical iceberg and estimates that as much as 94% of all illness is not actually reported to doctors.

Therefore much of our health is shaped by societal factors. However, the biomedical model argues that in fact many illnesses are natural, physical conditions. Hart notes that the human body is like a machine and that illness and disease happens in the body of an individual, not as part of society as a whole.

Marker's comments

AO1 – This gains up to **5** knowledge and understanding marks by showing a very clear understanding of the social construction of health throughout. Marks are gained for a clear definition in the introduction. There is sound knowledge of the social model and negative labelling as well as key terms such as clinical iceberg and the use of statistics to back up the points. There is also strong knowledge of studies/theory to back up the two arguments.

AO2 – The answer gains up to **3** marks as it shows a clear interpretation of the question and applies two good reasons backed up by the application of Marxism and writers Senior, Viveash and Last. There is also good interpretation of the question by identifying the difference between social construction and biological determinism.

AO3 – This gains up to **2** analysis marks in the overall concluding paragraph, making an analysis of the question by offering an alternative suggestion with the biomedical model. Marks are also gained for the use of Hart in an overall evaluation sentence.

[0][8] **8–10** Answers in this band will show good knowledge and understanding of relevant material on two reasons for the negative stigma attached to mental illness.

There will be two applications of relevant material, for example there is a lack of education or public understanding of many conditions; mental illness often becomes the master status of the individual.

There will be appropriate analysis/evaluation of two reasons, for example suggesting how the individual may face rejection or discrimination for their condition and lack of education on the condition.

4–7 Answers in this band will show a basic to reasonable knowledge and understanding of one or two examples of why there is a stigma attached to mental illness.

There will be some successful application of material from the item, for example developing the reasons as to why some conditions are misinterpreted by others.

There will be some analysis/evaluation.

1–3 Answers in this band will show limited knowledge and understanding of stigmatising mental illness.

There will be limited application of material from the item, for example some general discussion about examples of mental illnesses rather than linked to stigmatising the illness. Some material may be at a tangent to the question.

There will be limited or no analysis/evaluation.

0 No relevant points.

Indicative content

Answers may include the following and/or relevant points.

- Lack of education or public knowledge about the condition.
- Interactionist ideas on negative labelling of conditions, for example Goffman.
- Negative perception of receiving 'psychiatric treatment'.
- Misunderstanding of conditions such as depression.
- Some individuals suffer a disconnection from social life/isolation.
- Negative perception of some conditions through the mass media.

Top band answer

Maximum mark out of 10

3 marks for AO1: Knowledge and understanding

4 marks for AO2: Interpretation and application

3 marks for AO3: Analysis and evaluation

Human and medical understanding of mental illness has developed and improved rapidly in recent times. Despite this, there is still a stigma attached to it, meaning that mental illness is often viewed negatively or with a distinct caution and concern by others.

As stated in Item A, one reason for this is the lack of education or understanding of particular conditions, which often causes sufferers to be negatively labelled. Goffman studied mental institutions and found that they were often quick to judge a patient as unstable, crazy or exaggerate their condition. This caused the patient to actually become worse because of the constant reinforcement of the label to the point that they were unable to manage on their own outside the institution. Goffman claims that were there a better understanding of the conditions and how to deal with them, the patients' mental health could have improved rather than deteriorated, thereby reducing the overall stigma that often exists.

The second reason for the negative stigma is because of how others view the individual. Laing suggests that those with a history of mental illness are less likely to be accepted in education, relationships and in employment. The mental illness becomes their master status that others cannot see past. Goffman refers to this as the mortification of the self, whereby the person becomes stripped of their original personality and is left with a master status of a mentally ill person. The issue here is that others in society will often discriminate against those with such mental illnesses thereby increasing the stigma.

However, as mentioned in Item A, the provision for mental illness has improved significantly in the last 30 years; there is less shame and more social acceptance. This can be seen especially in the media reports on well-known celebrities and people of high social standing living with such conditions. Although some stigma remains, social attitudes towards mental illness are improving all the time.

Marker's comments

AO1 – This gains up to **3** knowledge and understanding marks by outlining a clear definition of what a stigma is. There is strong knowledge of educational issues and social issues as well as knowledge of terms such as labelling, mortification of self and master status. There is also use of key theorists.

AO2 – The answer gains up to **4** marks as it shows a clear interpretation of the question and applies two strong reasons. The first point applies and builds on the item well and the second point applies plenty of key terms in addition to discussion of the theorist Goffman. There is strong interpretation of the question throughout.

AO3 – This gains up to **3** analysis marks by clearly looking at the stigma of mental illness from two different angles applying Goffman for the first point and then Laing for the second. The concluding paragraph also gains marks by evaluating how attitudes towards mental illness have started to change and become more socially accepted.

0 9 **17–20** Answers in this band will show sound, conceptually detailed knowledge of a range of relevant material on gender, health and life chances. A sophisticated understanding of the question and of the presented material will be shown.

Appropriate material applied accurately and with sensitivity to the issues raised by the question.

Evaluation will be explicit and relevant. Evaluation may be developed, for instance by contrasting biological, cultural and socialisation factors including feminist theories in particular. Analysis will show clear explanation and draw appropriate and relevant conclusions.

13–16 Answers in this band will show accurate, broad and/or deep but incomplete knowledge. Understanding of a number of significant aspects of the question; good understanding of the presented material.

Application of the material is largely explicitly relevant to the question, though some material may be inadequately focused.

Some limited explicit evaluation and analysis, for example evaluating feminist views on patriarchy/domestic violence and/or some appropriate analysis, for example clear explanations with regard to employment issues.

9–12 Answers in this band will show a largely accurate knowledge but limited range and depth, for example a basic account of reasons why men and women live to different ages or a general account of the use of healthcare. Understanding of some limited but significant aspects of the question; superficial understanding of the presented material.

Applying listed material from the general topic area but with limited regard for its relevance to the issues raised by the question, or applying a narrow range of more relevant material.

Evaluation will take the form of a comparison of competing positions or one or two isolated points about globalisation. Analysis will be limited, with answers tending towards the descriptive.

5–8 Answers in this band will show limited undeveloped knowledge, for example two to three insubstantial points about gender or healthcare in general. Understanding only limited aspects of the question; simplistic understanding of the presented material.

Limited application of suitable material, and/or material often at a tangent to the demands of the question.

Very limited or no evaluation. Attempts at analysis, if any, are thin and disjointed.

1–4 Answers in this band will show a very limited knowledge, for example one to two very basic points about life chances or healthcare. Very little or no understanding of the question and of the presented material.

Significant errors, omissions, and/or incoherence in application of material.

No analysis or evaluation.

0 No relevant points.

Indicative content

Concepts and issues such as: biological – physicality, testosterone, oestrogen, childbirth, risk taking, mortality and morbidity rates; social – employment, division of labour, triple shift, manual work, drug and alcohol use, visiting GP, masculinity, showing emotion; structural factors – feminism linked to patriarchy/domestic violence/employment/medical profession. Also media campaigns, labelling and stigmatising illness. Theorists such as Oakley, Pahl, Blaxter, Bernard, and Doyal and Pennell.

Top band answer

Maximum mark out of 20

8 marks for AO1: Knowledge and understanding

6 marks for AO2: Interpretation and application

6 marks for AO3: Analysis and evaluation

As stated in Item B, statistics show that women live on average 5% longer than men do, although women are more likely to be sick and certainly more likely to visit a medical practitioner. There are a range of explanations for this but they broadly fall into categories of biological, social and structural, with each suggesting different reasons for the gender imbalance in health.

Biological theories are supported by the biomedical model of health which suggests that health and disease are natural and physical. Therefore this model would suggest that much of our gender differences in health patterns can be attributed to our genetic make-up. For example, women may suffer ill health in relation to menstruation, pregnancy and the menopause whereas men are more likely to suffer heart conditions that are more likely to impact life chances and longevity.

Hart states that physical symptoms are related to simple biology, so men as the stronger of the two sexes may be able to withstand harsher physical conditions. Testosterone levels may also provide the man with more strength to be able to cope with pain, while women may suffer more with certain health conditions such as post-natal depression due to the production of oestrogen hormones.

Many feminists disagree with this theory, however, and believe that gender differences in health are actually more social than biological. Nicholson, for example, believes that post-natal depression is related to social conditions and biologists are too quick to label the condition as a biological mental disorder. This could impact upon women in terms of promotion or being employed in prestigious jobs.

Marxist feminists such as Marsden attribute female ill health to the societal pressures of the triple shift whereby many women are expected to perform the roles of economic, domestic and emotional labour. Radical feminists support this claim and say that female ill health is brought on due to low social status, social isolation and the stress of childcare. These factors limit the life chances of women as they do not have time to focus on employment to the same degree as men.

Likewise, the social position may also explain why many men choose not to visit the doctor and therefore are also likely to get sick. Males are often expected by society to show signs of strength and dominance; an admission of illness may be considered a sign of weakness. Mac An Ghaill discusses the crisis of masculinity in that many men feel a pressure to maintain traditional masculine behaviours even when they are suffering. This shows that women are more likely to use health resources that increase their life chances.

This would also explain why suicide rates are so much higher for men than they are for women. It is estimated that around 75% of all suicides are carried out by men; this is often attributed to the societal pressure of being the breadwinner, especially at times of recession or redundancy. It is also thought that the societal norm for men to not show emotion, to not cry or show weakness also contributes to men bottling up their feelings rather than being open and expressive.

The structural theory relates to societal factors but looks more in depth at how societies are often stratified by power. Feminists point to the patriarchal nature of health care, for example life chances differ due to the fact that men are more likely to have higher positions in the medical world while women carry out the more caring but lower-paid positions.

Oakley continues this debate by saying that often midwives and nurses carry out subordinate roles. In other words it is often the female servant who is obeying the male doctor's instructions. Likewise, many positions in the world of scientific discovery of medicine and the supply of drugs are also dominated by men.

Radical feminists look at issues such as contraceptive pills, which can be deemed as patriarchal because they carry a health risk for the woman. Likewise third-wave feminists have discussed the social pressure on females to have plastic surgery to meet the unachievable ideals of attractiveness that are placed on women. They refer to this as the medicalisation of beauty. Evidence shows therefore that women are more likely to use health care for domestic reasons.

This does not explain why women live longer though. Supporters of men's rights issues in fact point to evidence that shows the health care system is actually more geared towards care for women, with 75% of all NHS workers and 90% of all nurses being female. This may also be a contributing factor in the reluctance of many men to seek medical assistance when they are ill.

In conclusion, there are many explanations for the different health patterns and life chances for men and women. Certainly, many of these factors are biological and therefore a natural process. However, many issues of health can clearly be related to the stereotypes and norms that society places on the expected behaviours for men and women. The provision and use of health care should be similar for both sexes but an analysis of research shows that this is far from the case.

Marker's comments

AO1 – This essay gains up to **8** knowledge and understanding marks as it demonstrates a very strong understanding of health and life chances for men and women. The essay has good knowledge of both the biomedical model, social and structural theory as well as applying a range of feminist theory: liberal, Marxist and radical. Understanding is shown through the use of key terms such as triple shift, subordinated roles and the crisis of masculinity.

AO2 – Up to **6** marks are gained for interpretation and application, first through building on the item in the introduction. The material, theories and evidence to support the arguments can be seen through the application of Hart, Marsden, Mac An Ghaill and Oakley to support the three lines of argument. There is very good interpretation and selection of relevant writers throughout.

AO3 – This essay gains up to **6** analysis marks by contrasting the biomedical, social and structural theories to explain gender difference in health. Analysis marks are also gained by comparing different feminist theories and also writers supporting male health rights. There are also evaluative marks gained in the final paragraph by stating how many health issues link to stereotypes.

Topic A4 – Work, Poverty and Welfare

10 **8–10** Answers in this band will show very good knowledge and understanding of globalisation and unemployment levels.

There will be two applications of relevant material, for example how immigrants often take on a range of lower paid/low skilled jobs or how global technology can lead to automation and pushing up employment levels.

There will be appropriate analysis, for example considering that globalisation can cause both a rise and a fall in unemployment.

4–7 Answers in this band will show a reasonable to good knowledge and understanding of globalisation and unemployment levels.

There will be one or two applications of relevant material, for example discussing how globalisation increases geographical mobility.

There will be some basic analysis.

1–3 Answers in this band will show limited knowledge and little or no understanding of the question or the material.

There will be limited focus on the question, for example there may be a drift into a general discussion of globalisation or unemployment but not linked together.

There will be limited or no analysis.

0 No relevant points.

Indicative content

Answers may include the following and/or other relevant points.

- Increased geographical mobility in a global society.
- More immigrants into a country/more emigration out of a country.
- Global technology can lead to automation.
- Global franchises can lead to local businesses closing.
- Online technology can cause individuals to lose jobs.
- Global market of jobs can lead to more opportunities outside the local economy.

Top band answer

Maximum mark out of 10

5 marks for AO1: Knowledge and understanding

3 marks for AO2: Interpretation and application

2 marks for AO3: Analysis and evaluation

Globalisation refers to the sharing of behaviours, practices and services on a worldwide scale, such as international brands and businesses like Coca-Cola or McDonald's infiltrating all countries across the world. The impacts of globalisation can have both a positive and negative effect on unemployment.

From a positive point of view, post-modernists such as Baudrillard believe that globalisation creates more opportunities for work and thus can lower unemployment rates. For instance, the advent of new media means that people can work remotely from anywhere as long as they have a good internet connection and therefore companies such as Google can be located in a variety of different countries with people of all nationalities working for them. Neophiliacs are researchers who believe that global new media can therefore offer far more job opportunities than ever before.

However, New Right theorists believe that globalisation actually has a negative impact on employment because it increases geographical mobility and immigration. They believe that immigrants can force the local-born residents out of jobs as they often fill the low-paid, low-skilled jobs that the working classes would previously have taken on. According to Murray, this process causes a growing underclass of people who become welfare dependent as they are either forced out of work due to immigration or by automation. This means that many jobs are taken over by developments in global technology, robots and computers that can replace human labour. Cultural pessimists also subscribe to this view: that new media actually pushes up unemployment rather than creating more opportunities.

Therefore, it is difficult to judge whether globalisation is having a positive or negative impact on unemployment. What is clear, however, is that it causes the job market to continually change, adapt and diversify. Traditional manual work seems to be on the decline but there is a huge increase in media-based service industries.

Marker's comments

AO1 – This gains up to **5** knowledge and understanding marks by showing a very clear understanding of globalisation and employment throughout. Marks are gained for a clear definition in the introduction. There is sound knowledge of employment opportunities and issues relating to the underclass as well as key terms such as geographical mobility, welfare dependency and automation. There is also strong knowledge of post-modernism and New Right theory to back up the two arguments.

AO2 – The answer gains up to **3** marks as it shows a clear interpretation of the question and applies two good reasons backed up by the application of writers such as Baudrillard and Murray. There is also good interpretation of the question by identifying the difference between positive and negative impacts of globalisation on employment.

AO3 – This gains up to **2** analysis marks in the overall concluding paragraph, making an analysis of the fact that the job market continually changes. Marks are also gained for evaluating that service industries are replacing manual work.

1 1 **8–10** Answers in this band will show good knowledge and understanding of relevant material on two ways in which voluntary aid can help the disadvantaged.

There will be two developed applications of material from the item, for example hostels and shelter for the homeless; offering emotional/welfare support for victims of abuse.

There will be appropriate analysis/evaluation of two reasons, for example suggesting how these groups often lack sufficient funding despite their good interests.

4–7 Answers in this band will show a basic to reasonable knowledge and understanding of one or two examples of voluntary aid groups and the benefits they offer.

There will be some successful application of material from the item, for example developing why these groups are needed alongside welfare and private provision.

There will be some analysis/evaluation.

1–3 Answers in this band will show limited knowledge and little to no understanding of one or two reasons for voluntary aid groups.

There will be limited application of material from the item. Some material may be at a tangent to the question, for example some general discussion about different types of groups rather than what they can provide as a service.

There will be little or no analysis.

0 No relevant points.

Indicative content

Answers may include the following and/or relevant points.

- Shelter and hostels for the homeless.
- Emotional support/counselling for victims of abuse.
- Church support groups for bereaved or sick individuals.
- Children's charities for the disaffected or ill.
- Volunteer groups for those with disabilities.
- Aid for those in LEDCs.

Top band answer

Maximum mark out of 10

3 marks for AO1: Knowledge and understanding

4 marks for AO2: Interpretation and application

3 marks for AO3: Analysis and evaluation

Voluntary groups refers to those organisations that are funded by charitable income with little to no state funding. They can provide a free service to individuals or at a subsidised low cost. As stated in Item A, these groups aim to help those with a range of needs such as the homeless, the elderly or the disabled.

One such example of a service these groups provide is with housing, by providing hostels and shelters for the homeless. These are frequently staffed by volunteers and therefore there is no cost for staff wages. These hostels also rely on the goodwill of local residents for food parcels and financial contributions. The Marxist Westergaard argues that these groups are essential as the welfare state has failed to reduce inequality between the rich and poor in society; the cost of living has risen so dramatically that the lower classes are priced out of both the house buying and even rental markets. However, the standard of accommodation is often of a very low quality and in deprived areas.

Another example of a disadvantaged group that can be helped is the elderly, through groups such as Age UK (formerly Help the Aged). Due to an ageing population, a larger percentage of the population are now elderly, meaning that more provision is required, particularly for those who require long-term, 24-hour care and provision. Once again, Marxists such as Resler believe that organisations such as Age UK are essential as state pensions offer a relatively low payout and the NHS is frequently overwhelmed and understaffed. Groups like Age UK offer an essential service for a very disadvantaged group, though finding volunteers and contributions to help the elderly is often problematic.

Despite the benefits that voluntary groups can offer, they are often struggling for financial injections and rely on the good nature of the public. Many of these organisations are finding it difficult to continue and do not have the regular income necessary to meet the demands of those that are disadvantaged.

Marker's comments

AO1 – This gains up to **3** knowledge and understanding marks by outlining a clear definition of what a voluntary organisation is. There is strong knowledge shown regarding helping the homeless and the elderly as well as the use of Marxism and key theorists.

AO2 – The answer gains up to **4** marks as it shows a clear interpretation of the question and applies two strong examples of provision from voluntary aid groups. Both points apply Marxist theory through the use of Westergaard followed by Resler for the second point. There is application of the item in the introduction and strong interpretation of the question throughout.

AO3 – This gains up to **3** analysis marks by clearly looking at voluntary organisations from two different angles, both applying Marxism but two clear reasons. The concluding paragraph also gains marks by evaluating how voluntary organisations are beneficial to those that use them but they are also in financial difficulties.

1 2 **17–20** Answers in this band will show sound, conceptually detailed knowledge of a range of relevant material on poverty rates in developing countries. A sophisticated understanding of the question and of the presented material will be shown.

Appropriate material will be applied accurately and with sensitivity to the issues raised by the question.

Analysis and evaluation will be explicit and relevant. Evaluation may be developed, for instance by contrasting the benefits of development with Marxist theory. Analysis will show clear explanation and draw appropriate and relevant conclusions.

13–16 Answers in this band will show accurate, broad and/or deep but incomplete knowledge. Understanding will be shown of a number of significant aspects of the question; reasonable understanding of the presented material.

Application of the material is largely explicitly relevant to the question, though some material may be inadequately focused.

Some limited explicit evaluation and analysis, for example looking at how development tends to benefit only the bourgeoisie.

9–12 Answers in this band will show a largely accurate knowledge but limited range and depth, for example a basic account of what happens economically when a country develops. Understanding will be shown of some aspects of the question; superficial understanding of the presented material.

Applying listed material from the general topic area but with limited regard for its relevance to the issues raised by the question, or applying a narrow range of more relevant material.

Evaluation will take the form of a comparison of competing positions or one or two isolated points about economic development. Analysis will be limited, with answers tending towards the descriptive.

5–8 Answers in this band will show limited undeveloped knowledge, for example two to three insubstantial points about development or Marxism in general. Understanding will be shown of only very limited aspects of the question; simplistic understanding of the presented material.

Limited application of suitable material, and/or material often at a tangent to the demands of the question.

Very limited or no evaluation. Attempts at analysis, if any, are thin and disjointed.

1–4 Answers in this band will show a very limited knowledge, for example one to two very basic points about developing countries. Very little or no understanding of the question and of the presented material.

Significant errors, omissions, and/or incoherence in application of material.

No analysis or evaluation

0 No relevant points.

Indicative content

Concepts and issues such as: globalisation/global development; post-modernity and trade; international trade; urbanisation; industrialisation; transnational corporations; demographics; industrial capitalism; dependency theory. Perspectives such as functionalism and post-modernism may be used alongside Marxism and New Right theory. Writers such as Lister, Alcock and Palmer may be applied.

Top band answer

Maximum mark out of 20

8 marks for AO1: Knowledge and understanding

6 marks for AO2: Interpretation and application

6 marks for AO3: Analysis and evaluation

As stated in Item B, the aim for many poor countries is to develop their economy so that that they can move out of poverty and improve the quality of life for those at the bottom. There are examples around the world of countries that have achieved this with great success. However, many sociologists believe that development simply causes the rich to get richer at the expense of the poor.

Post-modern theorists such as Bauman identify that globalisation and international trade means that it is easier for countries to develop and therefore reduce poverty rates. In the past many countries were isolated from international developments but now the advent of new technology and communication means that countries are increasingly interconnected and less detached from global developments.

Martell states that globalisation offers many opportunities for greater interaction and participation in societies throughout the world, for instance through the media and migration. This means that people from LEDCs have more opportunity to either move away for work or make connections with MEDCs through business and trade to help bring money into their home country. This view is criticised by writers such as Lister who see globalisation leading to increased powerlessness of the poor.

Functionalists also believe that inequality in developing countries provides the impetus for meritocracy and the desire to work hard. Davis and Moore state that people in developing countries become motivated by the status and power of more developed countries, meaning that individuals will work really hard to become socially mobile. Evidence of this can be seen in countries such as Kenya where Nairobi is becoming an increasingly powerful, global and technological city and the business hub for east Africa.

Likewise, New Right thinkers such as Saunders believe that this stratification of wealth is a good idea because inequality motivates people to work hard. He believes that developing countries become motivated by developed countries and this in turn encourages economic growth. As new businesses are set up in developing countries more opportunities are created for people and this causes poverty rates to fall.

There are many examples to support this theory: fewer people live in absolute poverty in the post-modern world as business opportunities and foreign aid have increased in even the most deprived of countries. However, many argue that if you measure poverty through relative poverty rather than absolute poverty then inequality in the developing countries has actually widened and got worse.

Traditional Marxist views disagree with the belief that as a country develops it reduces poverty. The reason for this is these countries follow the distinctive model of capitalism and for Marxists, capitalism is a flawed system based on the necessity to have inequality, greed and only serves self-interest. Although a country may come out of economic poverty under the capitalist system, closer inspection of the finances will only highlight inequality of wealth for the individuals.

Neo-Marxists such as Wright identify that as a country develops there is a growth of the middle classes which on the outside looks a positive transition. However, the development of this class is at the expense of the lower classes. This is because as more people have access to setting up businesses then they simply use the lower classes as cheap labour to increase their own profits.

Edgell discusses how there is a lack of social mobility in these instances; only a select few make it from the lower to the middle classes while the remainder in the proletariat live under the false dream that they too will have the opportunities to move up the social class ladder. This is often referred to as false class consciousness.

Singer notes that what actually occurs in developing countries is the exploitation of LEDCs in order to benefit MEDCs; he calls this dependency theory. This is where poor nations provide natural resources, cheap labour and opportunity markets for rich developed nations to exploit. The developing countries believe they are getting opportunities when in reality they are fuelling further wealth for the elite.

Prebisch therefore agrees with the statement in Item B that as a country becomes economically stable it simply causes the gap between rich and poor to become more polarised. By this he means that developing countries can improve their own economy but in turn they are benefiting the richer nations. Therefore the gap is never actually closing and, if anything, is widening.

Therefore, it may be fair to say that as a country develops it can reduce the amount of absolute poverty and provide more job opportunities to those who were previously unemployed. However, if we use relative poverty as a measurement then it is clear that the gap between the rich and poor in developing countries only seems to get wider as the country becomes more affluent.

Marker's comments

AO1 – This essay gains up to **8** knowledge and understanding marks as it demonstrates a very strong understanding of poverty rates and developing countries. The essay has good knowledge of a range of theories such as post-modernism, functionalism, New Right, Marxism and neo-Marxism. Understanding is shown through the use of key terms such as globalisation, social mobility, stratification, capitalism, exploitation and the polarisation of wealth.

AO2 – Up to **6** marks are gained for interpretation and application, first through building on the item in the introduction. The material, theories and evidence to support the arguments can be seen through the application of Bauman, Martell, Saunders, Wright, Edgell, Singer and Prebisch to support the two lines of argument for and against the statement. There is very good interpretation and selection of relevant writers throughout.

AO3 – This essay gains up to **6** analysis marks through contrasting evidence that poverty does decrease in the developing world against evidence against the statement. Analysis marks are also gained by comparing traditional sociological views with contemporary ones and left- versus right-wing thinking. There are also evaluative marks gained in the final paragraph by stating how the definition of poverty determines to what extent it can be measured.

Section B

Topic B1 – Beliefs in Society

1 3 **8–10** Answers in this band will show very good knowledge and understanding of religion linked to social class.

There will be two applications of relevant material, for example how religion offers salvation and hope from the current world; how religion can provide identity, cohesion and community in poorer areas.

There will be appropriate analysis, for example considering Marxist views that religion exploits those of a lower social standing.

4–7 Answers in this band will show a reasonable to good knowledge and understanding of religion and social class.

There will be one or two applications of relevant material, for example discussing functionalist views on consensus and unity.

There will be some basic analysis.

1–3 Answers in this band will show limited knowledge and understanding of the question or the material.

There will be limited focus on the question, for example there may be a drift into a general discussion of what religion offers but not linked to social class.

There will be limited or no analysis.

0 No relevant points.

Indicative content

Answers may include the following and/or relevant points.

• Functionalist views on consensus, community, identity.

• Salvation and hope of the afterlife.

• Cultural identity.

• A promise of social change.

• Provides charity and help to others.

• Marxist views on 'opium of the people'.

• Marxist views on false hope/class consciousness or justifying inequality.

Top band answer

Maximum mark out of 10

5 marks for AO1: Knowledge and understanding

3 marks for AO2: Interpretation and application

2 marks for AO3: Analysis and evaluation

As many parts of the world become more secular, it is noticeable that religion often remains a mainstay in the poorer nations and societies. Studies show that some of the poorest countries such as Niger, Bangladesh and Malawi are also on the list of the most religious countries on Earth. The reasons for poorer nations having a strong belief can be both positive and negative.

Functionalist writers such as Durkheim believe that religion can provide consensus, harmony and social cohesion, factors that can be essential in a poorer society. The church or place of worship is often the centre-point of many communities and it provides a place for everyone to come together at least once a week. At times of natural disasters or social unrest, particularly in poor areas, the place of worship is often the first point of contact for its congregation. Malinowski, for example, noted that religion is a tool to deal with emotional stress, social disorder and bereavement. Therefore religion can offer the poor a sense of direction and hope.

However, Marxists believe that religion actually offers false hope to its believers and therefore exploits the poor. Marx stated that religion is 'the opium of the people' and by this he meant that religion is often used like a drug for those in lower positions of society. One such example would be the promise of heaven as a reward for being good on Earth; for Marxists this justifies and legitimises living in poverty in this life as the believer holds on to the hope of a better afterlife. Marxists argue that religion can act as a conservative force in that it inhibits social change while maintaining inequality by continuing to offer a false promise to the poor.

Despite these views, evidence actually shows that the middle classes are more likely to be part of religious groups such as the Anglicans and Quakers. Bruce believes that this is because religion can fulfil the spiritual needs of people who have little financial pressure. Religion is also a key part of many of the richest nations on Earth such as in the Gulf region and therefore it would be inaccurate to say it is simply a mechanism for the poor.

Marker's comments

AO1 – This gains up to **5** knowledge and understanding marks by showing a very clear understanding of social class and religion throughout. There is sound knowledge of consensus and exploitation as well as key terms such as secular, social cohesion and conservative force. There is also strong knowledge of functionalist and Marxist theory to back up the two arguments.

AO2 – The answer gains up to **3** marks as it shows a clear interpretation of the question and applies two good reasons backed up by the application of writers such as Durkheim, Malinowski, Marx and Bruce. There is also good interpretation of the question by identifying the difference between positive and negative reasons for the lower classes adopting religion.

AO3 – This gains up to **2** analysis marks by comparing positive and negative reasons for religion among the poorer classes. Marks are also gained for evaluating how religion continues to remain common and popular among the middle classes too.

1 4 **8–10** Answers in this band will show good knowledge and understanding of relevant material on two ways in which religion acts as a conservative force.

There will be two developed applications of relevant material, for example it acts in a traditional manner in terms of morals and roles; it functions to preserve and stabilise a society (use of functionalist theory most likely to be applied here).

There will be appropriate analysis/evaluation, for example suggesting that religion can also act as an indicator for social change.

4–7 Answers in this band will show a basic, reasonable knowledge and understanding of one or two examples of religion acting as a conservative force.

There will be some successful application of material from the item, for example expanding on post-modern theory about why religion can be seen to be outdated in contemporary society.

There will be some basic analysis/evaluation.

1–3 Answers in this band will show limited knowledge and understanding of what is meant by a conservative force.

There will be limited focus on the question, for example some general discussion about religions unfocused to the question.

There will be little or no analysis.

0 No relevant points.

Indicative content

Answers may include the following and/or relevant points.

- Keeping traditional morals and norms.
- Offers stabilisation and security (functionalism).
- Restricts social change/justifies inequality/false class consciousness (Marxism).
- Rejects scientific development (post-modernism).
- Legitimises patriarchy (feminism).

Top band answer

Maximum mark out of 10

3 marks for AO1: Knowledge and understanding

4 marks for AO2: Interpretation and application

3 marks for AO3: Analysis and evaluation

The term conservative force means maintaining stability and tradition. For many people this is a major attraction of religion as it provides a constant in their life, with answers to their questions. Others, however, feel that religion being a conservative force does not allow for society to change or for human progression.

Functionalists such as Durkheim believe that religion can act as a conservative force by providing a collective conscience for the people. By this he means a shared set of beliefs, values and norms that can hold a society together. Durkheim believed that without religion a society would become less integrated and regulated; he referred to this as a state of anomie. What religion offers for functionalists is a sense of security in that it does not change; in a world of confusion, instability or mixed messages, the religious texts such as the Bible and the Qur'an offer a consistent message that provides a sense of security for many of its followers. However, many believe that religion needs to adapt and change with society; it cannot simply stand still as culture and attitudes change.

As stated in Item A, feminists also believe that religion acts as a conservative force but for them this is not a good thing. As a society progresses, it adapts and changes its mind on many social issues. For example, in the UK attitudes and laws on sexism, racism and homophobia have changed dramatically in just the last 50 years. Theorists such as De Beauvoir feel that religion does not adapt and change as social attitudes change, therefore leaving religious attitudes feeling antiquated and out of touch with contemporary society. This may explain why followers of religion are decreasing at a rapid rate in many nations. Some post-modernists do, however, show that religion can change, such as the recent acceptance of female priests.

Despite this, many theorists believe that religion can actually work as a mechanism for social change. In his study 'The Protestant Ethic and the Spirit of Capitalism' Weber suggested that the Calvinist religion was actually the catalyst for capitalism. His evidence shows the power of religion in having a major social impact on economics and society rather than simply acting as a conservative force.

Marker's comments

AO1 – This gains up to **3** knowledge and understanding marks by outlining a clear definition of what is meant by a conservative force. There is strong knowledge of both functionalist and post-modern theory as well as knowledge of different types of religions and use of key terms.

AO2 – The answer gains up to **4** marks as it shows a clear interpretation of the question and applies two strong reasons. Point one looks at a positive connotation, applying Durkheim's theories, and the second point applies and builds on the item using De Beauvoir as evidence. Therefore interpretation of the question is strong by looking at two alternative attitudes to religion being a conservative force.

AO3 – This gains up to **3** analysis marks by clearly looking at religion as a conservative force in both a positive and negative way and evaluating at the end of each paragraph. The concluding paragraph also gains marks by evaluating how religions can also be a force of change through Weber's study of the protestant ethic leading to capitalism.

1 5 **17–20** Answers in this band will show sound, conceptually detailed knowledge of a range of relevant material on the process of secularisation. A sophisticated understanding of the question and of the presented material will be shown.

Appropriate material will be applied accurately and with sensitivity to the issues raised by the question.

Analysis and evaluation will be explicit and relevant. Evaluation may be developed, for instance by contrasting where secularisation is and is not taking place or by evaluating the difficulty in measuring it. Analysis will show clear explanation and draw appropriate and relevant conclusions.

13–16 Answers in this band will show accurate, broad and/or deep but incomplete knowledge. Understanding will be shown of a number of significant aspects of the question; along with reasonable understanding of the presented material.

Application of the material is largely explicitly relevant to the question, though some material may be inadequately focused.

Some limited explicit evaluation and analysis, for example highlighting the rise in fundamentalism as a counterargument.

9–12 Answers in this band will show a largely accurate knowledge but limited range and depth, for example a basic account of what secularisation is with examples. Understanding will be shown of some aspects of the question; along with superficial understanding of the presented material.

Applying listed material from the general topic area but with limited regard for its relevance to the issues raised by the question, or applying a narrow range of more relevant material.

Evaluation will take the form of a comparison of competing positions or one or two isolated points about economic development. Analysis will be limited, with answers tending towards the descriptive.

5–8 Answers in this band will show limited undeveloped knowledge, for example two to three insubstantial points about what secularisation is or about religion in general. Understanding will be shown of only limited aspects of the question; along with simplistic understanding of the presented material.

Limited application of suitable material, and/or material often at a tangent to the demands of the question.

Very limited or no evaluation. Attempts at analysis, if any, are thin and disjointed.

1–4 Answers in this band will show a very limited knowledge, for example one to two very basic points about religion. Very little or no understanding of the question and of the presented material will be shown.

Significant errors, omissions, and/or incoherence in application of material.

No analysis or evaluation.

0 No relevant points.

Indicative content

Concepts and issues such as: post-modernism; globalisation; rationalisation; scientific developments; breakdown of the meta-narratives; religious attendance; disengagement; disillusion; privatised religion; religious pluralism; spiritual shopping; desacralisation. Writers may include Wilson, Glock and Stark, Berger, Lyotard, Bruce, Bauman, Davie, Weber, etc.

Top band answer

Maximum mark out of 20

8 marks for AO1: Knowledge and understanding

6 marks for AO2: Interpretation and application

6 marks for AO3: Analysis and evaluation

Wilson defines secularisation as a 'process whereby religious thinking, practice and institutions lose social significance'. Many theorists believe that there is an abundance of evidence for secularisation occurring based on religious commitment and importance. Others, however, state that religion is just going through a period of change or that religion is actually going through a process of resacralisation in that people are becoming more religious and spiritual.

To judge if secularisation is occurring and if it is inevitable, it is important to analyse those three distinctions as noted by Wilson: thinking, practice and institutional power. In terms of thinking, the founding fathers of sociology such as Comte and Weber predicted that secularisation was inevitable. Comte claimed that science would replace religion in the development of human thought.

Likewise, Weber stated that humans will go through a process of desacralisation and rationality. By this he meant that science and technology would replace magic and myth. A clear example of this is the breakdown of the meta-narratives. This means that science has explained away or disproved the big stories about life and creation in the major religious texts. However, many suggest that spirituality remains popular, seen in the rise of the New Age movement.

Bruce also notes that people think about religion far less in the post-modern world. Our lives are filled with many distractions that we prioritise over religion; this is particularly noticeable in northern Europe where surveys show a huge rise in atheism and agnosticism in the last decade.

As mentioned in the item, evidence also shows that there is also less practice of religion. A simple analysis of church statistics, for example, shows a huge fall in attendance over the last 50 years. Hewitt notes that the popularity of visiting a place of worship has fallen so much that many churches are becoming redundant or converted into storage, shops and carpet warehouses. It is estimated that UK churches have lost over 1 million attendees in the last two decades, though this does open up the question of whether people have lost their faith or just their attendance at a place of worship.

Bruce also notes how there is less practice on other levels too by highlighting the fall in baptisms, the reduction in church weddings and the distinct decline in the number of clergy, despite a growing population. Dobbelaere estimates that as little as 10% of the UK are members of the Christian church and many of those are not regular attendees either.

The Kendal project carried out by Heelas et al. is an indication of the rise of secularisation. The study of the town of 28,000 people was evidence of the general trend for people to be rather apathetic towards religion with low church attendance and little interest in faith. Although many people were involved in the likes of yoga and t'ai chi, this was not conducted in a religious sense but rather as a simple hobby or health activity.

In terms of institutional significance, again there is clear evidence that there has been a decrease in the power played by religious organisations in the general governance of society. Religion is no longer as important in politics and the economy; this is often referred to as disengagement as religion seems to become detached from the wider society. However, this certainly is not true in all countries where often religion and politics are still hugely intertwined.

Davie continues this argument by suggesting that societies are no longer guided by the kinds of collective moral codes of the church in politics and in schools. Likewise, the increasing acceptance of divorce and homosexuality is again further evidence of religions losing their grip on the control and power they once had in society.

Therefore, there is plenty of evidence of secularisation through rationalisation, desacralisation and disengagement. Despite this huge body of evidence, there are many that believe that this evidence is somewhat overstated and in fact there are plenty of examples of religions having something of a revival or resacralisation as it is often referred to.

Davie notes that the secularisation debate is too focused on the statistics and numbers of people attending places of worship and this does not necessarily mean religion is fading away but rather it is just adapting. Davie refers to this as 'believing without belonging'. In other words, for many people their faith has become privatised and personal; they still believe even if they are not overtly religious or a regular attendee at their place of worship.

Bellah backs up this theory by stating that religion has simply become more individualised in arguing that religion has not declined, it is simply that its form of expression has changed. Further evidence for this can be seen through religious pluralism. This means that there is more choice and diversity in religion than before. For example, many people moved away from mainstream religions in the 1970s but the New Age movement became popular; therefore, people had not turned their back on religion, but were simply searching for it on alternative paths.

There is also evidence of resacralisation, the belief that religion is becoming more popular; evidence of this can be seen in the rise of fundamentalism in recent years. Fundamentalism is when a religion advocates a strict observation of its traditional beliefs through asceticism. There are various examples of this occurring such as the rise of Christian fundamentalism in the USA or of Islam in Iraq. In other parts of the world spirituality and Buddhist practices such as meditation have also taken on global popularity.

Stark notes that religion is still relevant in many societies such as the UK as it remains the basis for moral codes and ethics such as the importance of the Ten Commandments in laws and policies. Likewise, national and school holidays are still centred around traditional Christian festivals such as Christmas and Easter.

Therefore, evidence seems to show that rather than fading away completely, religion is simply going through a change. Crockett and Voas state that British religion markets have become more competitive. There is now more choice in religion and therefore consumers have become spiritual shoppers, adopting several different practices from a range of religions.

In conclusion, it is very difficult to actually measure secularisation, partly because of the ambiguity in defining religion. If we were to simply analyse the major faiths then there is evidence for a decrease in popularity. However, if we were to use a more general definition of religion and spirituality then it would become more difficult to conclude that secularisation is inevitable.

It is also important to consider that the process of secularisation differs dramatically from country to country. Though there may be evidence of it in places such as Scandinavia, China and Japan, many parts of the world such as the Middle East maintain religion as a bedrock of society in order to maintain traditions and security. As Yip summarises, religion is in a constant state of transformation and therefore to judge if secularisation is occurring is a near impossible task.

Marker's comments

AO1 – This essay gains up to **8** knowledge and understanding marks as it demonstrates a very strong understanding of secularisation from the definitions in the introduction and throughout the essay. The essay has good knowledge of a range of theories such as post-modernism and Weberian theory and there is a wealth of sociological theory throughout the essay. Understanding is shown through the use of key terms such as desacralisation, resacralisation, rationalisation, privatised religion and fundamentalism.

AO2 – Up to **6** marks are gained for interpretation and application which builds on the evidence in the item. The material, theories and evidence to support the arguments can be seen through the application of Comte, Weber, Hewitt, Heelas, Bruce, Dobbelaere, Bellah, Yip and Crockett and Voas to support the two lines of argument for and against the statement. There is very good interpretation and selection of relevant writers throughout and interpretation marks are also awarded for referring to a range of religious practices.

AO3 – This essay gains up to **6** analysis marks through contrasting evidence that secularisation is both inevitable and that it is not. Analysis marks are also gained by comparing classic sociologists such as Comte and Weber to more contemporary writers such as Bruce. There are also evaluative marks throughout the essay and in the final paragraph, gained by stating how religion is constantly changing and transforming.

Topic B2 – Global Development

1 6 **8–10** Answers in this band will show very good knowledge and understanding of the features of urbanisation.

There will be two applications of relevant material, for example how urbanisation causes a densely populated environment and often overcrowding; how urbanisation can lead to the gentrification of a city.

There will be appropriate analysis, for example considering how urbanisation can have both positive and negative impacts for the city or the population.

4–7 Answers in this band will show a reasonable to good knowledge and understanding of urbanisation.

There will be one or two applications of relevant material, for example outlining how urbanisation impacts infrastructures and businesses.

There will be some basic analysis.

1–3 Answers in this band will show limited knowledge and little or no understanding of the question or the material.

There will be limited focus on the question, for example there may be a drift into a general discussion of why urbanisation happens rather than some of its features.

There will be limited or no analysis.

0 No relevant points.

Indicative content

Answers may include the following and/or relevant points.

- Overpopulation or densely populated conditions.
- Gentrification of certain areas.
- Gemeinschaft/gesellschaft of city communities.
- Homogenisation of city centres.
- Overcrowding of education/health services.
- Ex-urbanisation – wealthier residents move out of city.

Top band answer

Maximum mark out of 10

5 marks for AO1: Knowledge and understanding

3 marks for AO2: Interpretation and application

2 marks for AO3: Analysis and evaluation

Urbanisation refers to the movement of people from rural areas into the major cities. In 1800 around 3% of the population lived in towns and cities compared to the estimated 70% expected to live in urban areas by the year 2050. There are certain key characteristics to urbanisation.

One such feature is a dense population and overcrowding. Hoselitz states that people are attracted to the cities due to the appeal of work: major businesses, corporations and factories have long become centralised and therefore huge numbers of people swarm to these places of opportunity. This, however, does lead to issues of too many people in a confined space. In cities such as Beijing, Tokyo and London it has led to people living in very small, confined spaces at a very high cost. This overpopulation also has a huge impact on pollution and the health of the residents. However, it can be argued that as cities become more populous then they spread wider rather than maintaining the same size.

A second characteristic noticeable in many urban areas is the process of gentrification. This is when a rundown district is renovated and improved so that it conforms to more middle class tastes and ideals. Examples of this can be seen in London where previous council house areas have become very fashionable places to live. Marxists are often critical of this process as areas become gentrified at the expense of the working classes as they are often priced out of the market by the bourgeoisie who can afford to buy up the properties in these attractive urban locations. Despite this, there are still many areas that remain as slums or ghettos as opposed to experiencing gentrification.

There are, however, many benefits to urbanisation too. Tönnies states that many cities contain gemeinschaft and gesellschaft which basically means a sense of community and society. These densely populated areas often drive people to live, work and socialise together in close proximity.

Marker's comments

AO1 – This gains up to **5** knowledge and understanding marks by showing a very clear understanding of urbanisation throughout, including a sound definition in the introduction. There is strong knowledge of overcrowding and gentrification as well as key terms such as centralised, bourgeoisie, gemeinshaft and gesellschaft. There is also good knowledge of sociologists, a statistic and Marxist theory to back up the two arguments.

AO2 – This answer gains up to **3** marks as it shows a clear interpretation of the question and applies two good reasons backed up by the application of writers such as Hoselitz and Tönnies. There is also good interpretation of the question by identifying the difference between how a city can become too busy compared to becoming gentrified.

AO3 – This gains up to **2** analysis marks through evaluation at the end of the paragraphs and in the final paragraph by identifying that there are also positives to urbanisation and also using a sociologist and key terms to support this evaluative point.

1 7 **8–10** Answers in this band will show good knowledge and understanding of relevant material on two ways in which education can act as a tool for development.

There will be two developed applications of material from the item, for example that education participation reduces infant mortality and poor child health; education provides an increase in participation in decision-making processes.

There will be appropriate analysis and evaluation of two reasons, for example suggesting that education relates to quality and longevity of life or that education is not always delivered equally.

4–7 Answers in this band will show a basic to reasonable knowledge and understanding of one or two examples of education as a tool for development.

There will be some successful application of material from the item, for example expanding on the political importance of education.

There will be some analysis/evaluation.

1–3 Answers in this band will show limited knowledge and little to no understanding of how education can improve a society.

There will be limited focus on the question, for example some general discussion about education but not how it can act as a force for change.

There will be little or no analysis/evaluation.

0 No relevant points.

Indicative content

Answers may include the following and/or relevant points.

- Increased participation in decision-making processes.
- Improved understanding of health and wellbeing.
- Better understanding of disease and contamination.
- Providing specialised skills in order to complete certain jobs.
- Providing values, attitudes and status to individuals.

- Can act as a unifying force, encouraging help to others.

- Can increase the prospect of social mobility.

Top band answer

Maximum mark out of 10

3 marks for AO1: Knowledge and understanding

4 marks for AO2: Interpretation and application

3 marks for AO3: Analysis and evaluation

Rostow's model for development identifies that education is both key and necessary for a country to enhance and improve itself. Indeed the most progressive countries in the world have a strong education system at their core. This is a view shared by sociological perspectives such as functionalism and modernist theory.

Functionalists believe that education can work as a unifying force by giving people the basic skills, values and attitudes required to progress. For example, a better education on health and well-being has been key in reducing infant mortality and child illness. Durkheim stated that for a society to be stable it needed strong institutions in the form of the family, education and religion. Education is vital because it trains each new generation with the functional prerequisites required to survive and develop. As stated in Item A, education breeds a new workforce for the future. However, this does not account for some places experiencing very high unemployment.

When New Labour came into power in 1997 they also saw the importance of education as they believed that it gave people the opportunity to obtain achieved status – this means that educational qualifications increase and employment opportunities improve. More importantly they believed that opportunities in education are empowering for those groups in society that may previously have been excluded from the possibility of social mobility, such as the poor and women. Educational opportunities therefore may contribute to overcoming class, ethnic and religious differences in a country. Despite this, feminist researchers argue that there is still gender inequality in employment.

As stated in the item however, Marxists argue that education can only become a tool for development if it is fair and equally delivered to all. They note that the unfairness of education between state and private schools means that education only operates as a tool of development for those in the ruling classes. The evidence for this shows that indeed many working class students fail in education and leave without qualifications, even in developed countries.

Marker's comments

AO1 – This gains up to **3** knowledge and understanding marks by showing a good understanding of education and development. There is strong knowledge of functionalist, modernist and Marxist theory as well as the use of key sociological writers.

AO2 – The answer gains up to **4** marks as it shows a clear interpretation of the question and applies two strong reasons, each backed up with different evidence. Point one applies Durkheim's theory; the second point applies reference to New labour. The conclusion applies Marxism developed from the item; therefore interpretation of the question is strong throughout.

AO3 – This gains up to **3** analysis marks by contrasting two positives of education with the Marxist view. The concluding paragraph also gains marks by evaluating how education often still fails those students from the lower classes.

1 8 **17–20** Answers in this band will show sound, conceptually detailed knowledge of a range of relevant material on the positives and negatives of aid. Sophisticated understanding of the question and of the presented material will be shown.

Appropriate material will be applied accurately and with sensitivity to the issues raised by the question.

Analysis and evaluation will be explicit and relevant. Evaluation may be developed, for instance by contrasting the benefits and issues of aid backed up by sociological perspectives (functionalism, New Right, Marxism, etc). Analysis will show clear explanation and draw appropriate and relevant conclusions.

13–16 Answers in this band will show accurate, broad and/or deep but incomplete knowledge. Understanding will be shown of a number of significant aspects of the question; reasonable understanding of the presented material.

Application of the material is largely explicitly relevant to the question, though some material may be inadequately focused.

Some limited explicit evaluation, for example highlighting how aid promotes westernised culture only or serves the interests of capitalism.

9–12 Answers in this band will show a largely accurate knowledge but limited range and depth, for example a basic account of examples of aid developing countries. Understanding will be shown of some aspects of the question; superficial understanding of the presented material.

Applying listed material from the general topic area but with limited regard for its relevance to the issues raised by the question, or applying a narrow range of more relevant material.

Evaluation will take the form of a comparison of competing positions or one or two isolated points about aid and development. Analysis will be limited, with answers tending towards the descriptive.

5–8 Answers in this band will show limited undeveloped knowledge, for example two to three insubstantial points about what aid is rather than the strengths and limitations. Understanding will be shown only of very limited aspects of the question; simplistic understanding of the presented material.

Limited application of suitable material, and/or material often at a tangent to the demands of the question.

Very limited or no evaluation. Attempts at analysis, if any, are thin and disjointed.

1–4 Answers in this band will show a very limited knowledge, for example one to two very basic points about aid or development. Very little or no understanding of the question and of the presented material.

Significant errors, omissions, and/or incoherence in application of material.

No analysis or evaluation.

0 No relevant points.

Indicative content

Concepts and issues such as: neo-liberalism; modernisation theories; global economies; economic development; international trade; infrastructures; fair trade movement; NGOs/charity/voluntary aid; bilateral/multilateral aid; investment gaps; capitalist/westernised regimes; dependency culture; New Right theory; neo-Marxism. Writers such as Hayter, Sachs, and Cohen and Kennedy may be applied.

Top band answer

Maximum mark out of 20

8 marks for AO1: Knowledge and understanding

6 marks for AO2: Interpretation and application

6 marks for AO3: Analysis and evaluation

Aid can be given by countries in different forms, the most common being bilateral and multilateral aid plus provision from non-governmental organisations. The United Nations suggests that MEDCs should give around 0.7% of their GDP to LEDCs and in theory this should be a good model for sharing wealth. It is felt by many sociologists, however, that this model of aid actually causes more harm than good.

As stated in Item B, New Right theorists believe that aid simply creates a dependency culture – this means that countries become reliant on the money rather than standing on their own two feet. Murray suggests less-developed countries can start to view aid as a right rather than as a safety net or last resort. He believes that countries do not strive to progress if they are simply being given money as free handouts.

This view is also supported by neo-liberals who feel that aid has a negative impact on the free market. They believe that trade and business need to work on the basis of enterprise and investment, therefore aid disrupts this as it is money given to a country without the creative enterprise from the individuals in that society. This does, however, take a rather pessimistic view of aid.

Neo-Marxists also highlight the issues of aid but from a different angle; they believe that aid simply acts as a tool to serve capitalism. Urry argues that aid is tied up with certain conditions and interdependencies – one such example is that aid is often given to countries in exchange for cheap labour or free trade. This allows developed countries to import and export goods without trade or custom levies and thus exploit the developing country.

A further example of this can be seen in bilateral aid which often requires the LEDC to buy goods from the MEDC or employ technical experts from the developed country. Some neo-Marxists go as far as calling this a method of blackmail as the developing country only receives its aid by subscribing to unfair conditions first. However, many LEDCs welcome these ventures as a form of opportunity.

Hayter is also critical of this approach to aid as she feels it is a way of western societies politically influencing poorer nations with their viewpoints and stances on issues. This can cause homogenisation of values whereby western morals are forced on to a country at the expense of their own traditional views. Though this has happened in many places in the past, it is certainly not evident throughout the world.

Therefore, aid can often become more about trade and self development of the country offering it rather than an altruistic gesture or donation. Bauer argues that historically, when aid has been given directly to countries, the ruling elites have simply used it to consolidate their power and continue high levels of corruption.

Despite this however, as mentioned in the item, without this aid many of the developing countries could actually be in a far worse situation than they are already, and many of these contributions are given as an act of goodwill.

Countries such as Sweden, Netherlands and Norway have consistently hit the UN target of contributing 0.7% of their GDP. The UN have stated that this target would contribute to reductions of overall levels of poverty, give more access to safe drinking water and inject much needed money into the slums of some of the poorest nations on Earth. Therefore, there are various measurements of success for bilateral aid.

In terms of multilateral aid, international bodies such as the World Bank and UNESCO are offering essential grants and loans. Rather than causing a dependency culture it could be argued that these organisations are simply offering a leg up or starting platform for societies to then continue under their own steam.

Likewise, it is difficult to criticise non-government organisations such as Oxfam and Christian Aid, as their intentions to help others are done through goodwill and the charity of the general public. These donations are often referred to as acts of philanthropy, which means the desire to promote the welfare of others, expressed especially by the generous donation of money to good causes.

Although modernisation theorists see some faults in aid they do believe that it can have a positive trickle down effect in that money from the richer nations can work its way down eventually to help those nations that most need it. This in turn means that many developing countries experience growth and success.

To measure progress the human development index (HDI) can show a clear progression and improvement for some countries in terms of life expectancy, education levels and living standards. Palacios highlights, for example, that life expectancy in the 20th century rose from 50 to 66 years and much of this can be attributed to the importance of aid.

In conclusion, it is difficult to judge whether aid actually causes more harm than good as there are many examples of countries that have used aid to their advantage and raised their overall living standards. Aid is also often given out of compassion and a desire to help others, particularly money donations from the general public.

However, what is clear is that this money is often misused or falls into the wrong hands to fuel corruption. Perhaps then the issue is not the aid itself but rather the way in which it is managed and monitored and it is this that needs to change in order to improve overall development.

Marker's comments

AO1 – This essay gains up to **8** knowledge and understanding marks as it demonstrates a very strong understanding of aid including good examples in the introduction and then throughout the essay. The essay has good knowledge of theory such as neo-Marxism and modernisation theory. Understanding is also shown through the use of key terms such as bilateral and multilateral aid, homogenisation, philanthropy and corruption.

AO2 – Up to **6** marks are gained for interpretation and application that build on the evidence in the item straight away. The material, theories and evidence to support the arguments can be seen through the application of Murray, Urry, Hayter, Bauer and Palacios to support the two lines of argument for and against the statement. There is very good interpretation and selection of relevant writers throughout and interpretation marks are also awarded for referring to a range of different types of aid provision.

AO3 – This essay gains up to **6** analysis marks through clearly contrasting evidence that aid is beneficial or not. Analysis marks are also gained by comparing the Marxist and modernist approaches and attitudes to aid and through evaluation at the end of paragraphs. There are also evaluative marks gained in the final paragraph by stating how the management of aid may be more of an issue than the money itself.

Topic B3 – The Media

1 9 **8–10** Answers in this band will show very good knowledge and understanding of news values.

There will be two applications of relevant material, for example extraordinariness in terms of how unexpected, rare or unpredictable the event is; threshold, the size and scale of the event or number of people affected.

There will be appropriate analysis, for example by reflecting on some of the limitations of the news value.

4–7 Answers in this band will show a reasonable to good knowledge and understanding of news values.

There will be one or two applications of relevant material, for example outlining how news values relate to the importance of the personality impacted.

There will be some basic analysis.

1–3 In this band answers will show limited knowledge and understanding of news values.

There will be limited focus on the question, for example there may be a drift into a general discussion of how the news is presented rather than linked to the values.

There will be limited or no analysis.

0 No relevant points.

Indicative content

Answers may include the following and/or relevant points.

- Extraordinariness – to what extent is the event surprising?

- Size/threshold – how many people does the event impact upon?

- Unambiguity – the event is easy to understand and follow.

- Elitism – does the event impact an important person or country?

- Narrative – does the story have strong characters (good vs evil)?

- Negativity – death and tragedy are often exciting and dramatic to the public.

Top band answer

Maximum mark out of 10

5 marks for AO1: Knowledge and understanding

3 marks for AO2: Interpretation and application

2 marks for AO3: Analysis and evaluation

Chibnall defines news values as the criteria of relevance that guide the reporter's choice and construction of newsworthy stories. In other words, media outlets are aware that there are certain criteria and factors that cause a news story to generate more interest and greater numbers of people to follow it.

One such example is the size and scale of the event that has occurred, the theory being that the larger the event, the more newsworthy it becomes. A simple example can be seen in the reporting of disasters. The news media is always keen to inform the public of the rising death rate – this seems to tap into the curious nature of its followers and higher death rates result in more media attention. Size may also be the reason why the media often generates moral panics. Cohen suggests that the media often exaggerates or amplifies acts of deviance as it is fully aware that making out an event is huge or impacting upon a lot of people increases its popularity. This of course does not account for the popularity of local news.

A second example of a news value is to be unambiguous. This means that the news item should be easy to follow. Evidence shows that simple, clear and basic issues are more likely to be followed by the general public. An example of this is in stories regarding war, where the production paints a very clear picture of who is good and who is bad. Post-modernists have stated that much of our news now contains throwaway knowledge; for example major news stories on celebrity breakups or gossip about soap opera characters. News productions are aware that simple stories attract a larger number of viewers, although it can be argued that some media specialises in more highbrow news.

There are, however, a whole range of other news values beyond these two: Galtung suggests issues such as frequency and continuity are important; Lanson and Stephens believe that there needs to be an educational weight or importance behind an event; while Chibnall gives evidence that often something as basic as sex and titillation draws in the viewers.

Marker's comments

AO1 – This gains up to **5** knowledge and understanding marks by showing a very clear understanding of news values throughout including a sound definition in the introduction. There is strong knowledge of size/scale and unambiguity as well as key terms such as exaggeration, throwaway knowledge and titillation. There is also good knowledge of sociologists and post-modern theory to back up the two arguments.

AO2 – This answer gains up to **3** marks as it shows a clear interpretation of the question and applies two good clear news values. The first applies terms from Cohen and the second applies post-modern theory. The final paragraph also shows further interpretation of what news values are.

AO3 – This gains up to **2** analysis marks through evaluation at the end of each paragraph and in the final paragraph by identifying several different news values, each backed up with a key term and a supporting sociologist.

2 0 **8–10** Answers in this band will show good knowledge and understanding of relevant material on two reasons for the under-representation of ethnic minorities in the media.

There will be two applications of material from the item, for example analysing the idea of the white gaze; ethnocentric ownership or production of the media.

There will be appropriate analysis/evaluation of two factors, for example incorporating post-modern/pluralist theory as to how attitudes and representations are changing in contemporary media.

4–7 Answers in this band will show a basic to reasonable knowledge and understanding of one or two examples of under-representation of ethnic minorities in the media.

There will be some successful application of material from the item, for example expanding on the reasons behind low representation in television advertisements.

There will be some analysis/evaluation.

1–3 Answers in this band will show limited knowledge and understanding of ethnic under-representation in the media.

There will be limited focus application of material from the item. Some material may be at a tangent to the question, for example some general discussion about misrepresentation rather than under-representation.

There will be little or no analysis.

0 No relevant points.

Indicative content

Answers may include the following and/or relevant points.

- Carrington's white gaze theory.
- Ethnocentric ownership or production of media.
- Gilroy's discredited theory.
- Hyper-reality theory applied to ethnicity.
- Baudrillard's simulacra theory applied to ethnicity.
- Reference to ethnic minorities only used as tokenism.

Top band answer

Maximum mark out of 10

3 marks for AO1: Knowledge and understanding

4 marks for AO2: Interpretation and application

3 marks for AO3: Analysis and evaluation

Despite the growing numbers of ethnic minorities in countries such as the UK and the USA, there is still evidence to show that these groups are under-represented in the media. Many of the reasons for this can be related to both the ownership of the mass media and also in terms of how many forms of media are produced.

In terms of ownership, studies show that big media corporations on the whole are owned by wealthy, middle class, white males. This has become even more evident since the increase of media concentration whereby more and more smaller media companies are being bought out and taken over by the richest media superpowers. This can lead to what Sumner calls 'ethnocentric media'. This means that the news tends to cover stories that focus on the majority group in society and presents from the viewpoint of that major ethnic group. As stated in Item A, this could cause an issue with regard to under-representation. However, this has changed significantly in some places, such as the UK.

A second issue for the under-representation of ethnic minorities can be seen through Carrington's 'white gaze' theory. This is the view that the media looks at stories though the eyes of the white majority group. This often leads to black groups only really being represented in stereotypical genres such as sport and music. Gilroy extends this argument by describing ethnic minority under-representation as 'otherness', in that representation of these groups highlights differences in terms of language, religion and family life. Therefore ethnic minority coverage only seems to exist in small, stereotypical depictions, though this is gradually changing, especially in mainstream television shows.

However, it must be noted that representation of ethnic minorities has increased significantly in the last two decades, especially in examples of presenters on news programmes and major acting roles. Although far from equal, there have been huge strides made in the post-modern era to redress the balance of representation in comparison to the past.

Marker's comments

AO1 – This gains up to **3** knowledge and understanding marks by showing a good understanding of ethnicity in the media. There is strong knowledge of ownership and the white gaze as well as key terms such as ethnocentricity, stereotyping and otherness, all backed up by sociologists.

AO2 – The answer gains up to **4** marks as it shows a clear interpretation of the question and applies two strong reasons each backed up with a different theory. Point one applies the item and uses the theorist Sumner as evidence; the second point applies ideas from Gilroy. The concepts and evidence throughout demonstrate good interpretation.

AO3 – This gains up to **3** analysis marks by contrasting two very different reasons for under-representation, using evaluation at the end of the paragraphs. The concluding paragraph also gains marks by stating that representation is increasing and also by evaluating that progress in this area is being made.

2 1 **17–20** Answers in this band will show sound, conceptually detailed knowledge of a range of relevant material on the representation of social classes in the media. A sophisticated understanding of the question and of the presented material will be shown.

Appropriate material will be applied accurately and with sensitivity to the issues raised by the question.

Analysis and evaluation will be explicit and relevant. Evaluation may be developed, for instance by contrasting the Marxist and pluralist views on representation and applying post-modern theory too. Analysis will show clear explanation and draw appropriate and relevant conclusions.

13–16 Answers in this band will show accurate, broad and/or deep but incomplete knowledge. Understanding will be shown of a number of significant aspects of the question; reasonable understanding shown of the presented material.

Application of the material is largely explicitly relevant to the question, though some material may be inadequately focused.

Some limited explicit evaluation, for example analysing and assessing the Marxist view on class and media representations.

9–12 Answers in this band will show a largely accurate knowledge but limited range and depth, for example a basic account of class representation in the media. Understanding will be shown of some aspects of the question; superficial understanding shown of the presented material.

Applying listed material from the general topic area but with limited regard for its relevance to the issues raised by the question, or applying a narrow range of more relevant material.

Evaluation will take the form of a comparison of competing positions or one or two isolated points about aid and development. Analysis will be limited, with answers tending towards the descriptive.

5–8 Answers in this band will show limited undeveloped knowledge, for example two to three insubstantial points about higher class representation in the media. Understanding will be shown of only very limited aspects of the question; simplistic understanding shown of the presented material.

Limited application of suitable material, and/or material often at a tangent to the demands of the question.

Very limited or no evaluation. Attempts at analysis, if any, are thin and disjointed.

1–4 Answers in this band will show a very limited knowledge, for example one to two very basic points about media or social class. Very little or no understanding shown of the question and of the presented material.

Significant errors, omissions, and/or incoherence in application of material.

No analysis or evaluation.

0 No relevant points.

Indicative content

Concepts and issues such as: high/mass/popular culture; stereotyping; representations; marginalisation; invisible culture; Marxism and neo-Marxism; cultural capital; misrepresentation; hyper-reality; reference to Glasgow University Media Group (GUMG) studies on representation; labelling theory. Theorists such as Medhurst, Baudrillard, and Glennon and Butsch may be applied.

Top band answer

Maximum mark out of 20

8 marks for AO1: Knowledge and understanding

6 marks for AO2: Interpretation and application

6 marks for AO3: Analysis and evaluation

It has long been suggested by Marxist sociologists in particular that media production and presentation tend to work in the interest of the higher classes, in that there is a certain amount of bias towards how these groups are portrayed compared to lower class groups. However, as mentioned in Item B, the advent of new media and reality television has opened the door to far more representation of lower classes.

The Glasgow University Media Group (GUMG) conducted a large-scale piece of research in the 1980s and found that the bourgeoisie are presented as the innocent and conformist groups while the proletariat are frequently depicted as a source of trouble. It was concluded that the media perpetuates this view to ensure the dominance of a capitalist ideology. This may now be seen as rather outdated however, as working class representation has increased significantly in recent years.

Neo-Marxists continue this argument by identifying that the majority of editors and executives are middle class, and the middle classes are more likely to appear on dramas and news programmes as well as in serious television and historical costume dramas. Likewise, the working classes are frequently marginalised into limited or stereotypical soap opera roles in many shows, though this may not necessarily be the case in all productions. Others, however, believe that many of these shows are an accurate portrayal of real life.

Hall believes that this misrepresentation reinforces perceptions of class identities. It can be extremely damaging to have the middle classes always presented positively and the working classes in a negative light. Real evidence of this perception came in the form of Medhurst's study in the late 1990s that showed how The Royle Family, a comedy show about a benefit claiming family in the north of England, was indeed considered an accurate portrayal of working class life by its viewers.

Further evidence of this view comes from a study by Glennon and Butsch which argued that the majority of working class fathers are portrayed as stupid or comical and a simple source of fun for the audience to laugh at. They also identified that manual workers were only represented in 4% of sitcoms even though 36% of all American families have a manual worker as a head of the household.

Ehrenreich concludes that media representations boil down to very simple and obvious stereotypes and that this silences the working class voices, making them both literally and metaphorically dumb. However, it must be noted that many of these studies were conducted in the 1980s and 1990s and there is plenty of evidence to say that the media has gone through huge developments and changes in the last two decades.

Post-modernists such as Baudrillard believe that it is now far more difficult to assess whether the media presents social class accurately or not because we have become so media saturated that representations are hugely diverse. Hyper-reality theory suggests that what we often see in terms of social class may actually be a true representation but simply magnified and overly enhanced.

This idea of media saturation is also backed up by pluralist writers who believe that the public now has access to a plethora of media representations in many formats and forms. The narrow and stereotypical views on television 30 years ago were restricted to a few television stations; now the number of outlets for representation is huge.

Neophiliacs support this view that new media has given a voice to a wider number of people. In the past it would only be the elite and most powerful who could share their opinions but now social media sites such as Twitter, YouTube and Facebook have allowed the general public from all walks of life to put out their views into the world.

Negroponte takes an optimistic attitude to digital media too, as he believes one of the benefits is decentralisation. By this he means that more and more power is being taken away from the major corporations as the general public have more of an outlet to express views, giving empowerment to people of all social class backgrounds. Surowiecki agrees that the global flow of the new media weakens the state's hold over individuals and ideas.

As mentioned in Item B, evidence of the rise in popularity of low or mass culture can be seen in the impact and magnitude of reality television over the last 15 years which has grown significantly in that time period. Post-modernist writers have often referred to this type of entertainment as providing the viewer with 'throw-away knowledge' in that the programmes are often simple to follow, repetitive and not educationally demanding. They provide a huge source of entertainment though as they pull in huge viewing figures – meaning they would be considered a key part of mass culture.

Therefore, it is very difficult to say that the media now only reflects the interests of the higher classes. This may have been true 30 years ago when we only had a limited number of media outlets controlled by middle class executives. Now however, new media in the post-modern world is so diverse, fragmented and global that it allows a far wider spread of representation from people of all social backgrounds.

The media has become more individualised and decentralised. In a media-saturated world we are now able to pick up and consume media in any place, at any time and in every form from low, high, mass and global culture. The media is no longer simply limited to being under the control of the bourgeoisie.

Marker's comments

AO1 – This essay gains up to **8** knowledge and understanding marks as it demonstrates a very strong understanding of social class and representation. The essay has good knowledge of theory such as Marxism, neo-Marxism, neophiliac theory, post-modernism as well as the GUMG. Understanding is also shown through the variety of key terms such as capitalism, marginalisation, stereotyping, hyper-reality, media saturation and decentralisation.

AO2 – Up to **6** marks are gained for interpretation and application which builds on the evidence in the item within the introduction. The material, theories and evidence to support the arguments can be seen through the application of Medhurst, Glennon and Butsch, Ehrenreich, Baudrillard and Surowiecki to support the two lines of argument for and against the statement. Interpretation marks are also awarded for referring to a range of different types of media such as television, newspapers and social media rather than simply focusing on one format of media production.

AO3 – This essay gains up to **6** analysis marks by clearly contrasting evidence both for and against the statement. Analysis marks are also gained by comparing different sociological perspectives that are either positive or negative in their views on representation. There are also evaluative marks to be gained in the penultimate paragraph by discussing changes in the last 30 years and in the final paragraph by emphasising the decentralisation of media.

Topic B4 – Stratification and Differentiation

2 2 **8–10** Answers in this band will show very good knowledge and understanding of defining a person's social class.

There will be two applications of relevant material, for example the use of their language (elaborated or restricted); their cultural capital, hobbies and pastimes (high or low culture).

There will be appropriate analysis, for example referring to the difficulty of defining social class.

4–7 Answers in this band will show a reasonable to good knowledge and understanding of defining social class.

There will be one or two applications of relevant material, for example outlining friendship groups or who the person spends time with.

There will be some basic analysis.

1–3 Answers in this band will show limited knowledge and little or no understanding of defining social class.

There will be limited focus on the question, for example there may be a drift into discussion of occupation or simply defining different types of social class.

There will be limited or no analysis.

0 No relevant points.

Indicative content

Answers may include the following and/or relevant points.

- Bernstein's language codes (elaborated or restricted).
- Bourdieu's cultural capital in terms of attitudes and behaviours.
- High/low culture in terms of consumption of media and hobbies.
- Clothing – could be linked to branding/styles.
- Housing/location/peer groups.

Top band answer

Maximum mark out of 10

5 marks for AO1: Knowledge and understanding

3 marks for AO2: Interpretation and application

2 marks for AO3: Analysis and evaluation

Social class refers to a group of people with similar levels of wealth, influence and status, with examples being working, middle and upper class. Sociologists tend to judge the social class of a person by their occupation and income; however, the social class of a person can also be defined by several other characteristics.

One such indicator of class is the use of language. Bernstein suggested that those with a middle/upper class accent use an elaborated code while those from the lower classes use a restricted code. He notes that the elaborated code uses a wider vocabulary, fewer swear words and an elongation of the vowel sounds. This is often referred to as the Queen's English or received pronunciation. The working class restricted code language is more likely to have a stronger regional accent whereby local dialect, abbreviations, slang and profanities are more present. Bernstein said that people are judged and stereotyped on their use of language as many people relate the elaborated code to intelligence.

A second judgement of class can be measured by what Bourdieu calls cultural capital. This refers to the manners and behaviours of an individual such as their hobbies, intellect, style of speech, dress or physical appearance. Bourdieu states that people are frequently judged by their cultural capital, for example high culture activities such as going to the opera or listening to classical music suggest a weight of intellect; likewise, stereotypes are often linked to the wearing of certain perceived working class clothes such as tracksuits and sportswear. Class can therefore be defined to a certain extent by appearance and pastimes.

However, it is often suggested that it is far more difficult to judge class in a post-modern society where behaviours and accents are becoming more homogenised. There is also a growing middle class and more people being university educated and so the distinction between the working and middle classes is arguably more difficult to measure than it was before.

Marker's comments

AO1 – This gains up to **5** knowledge and understanding marks by showing a very clear understanding of social class starting with a sound definition and examples in the introduction. There is strong knowledge of language codes and cultural capital as well as key terms such as elaborated/restricted code, stereotyping and homogenisation. There is also good knowledge of sociologists to back up the two arguments.

AO2 – This answer gains up to **3** marks as it shows a clear interpretation of the question and applies two good examples of defining social class. The first applies terms and theory from Bernstein and the second terms and theory from Bourdieu. Interpretation of the question is strong through the application of well-known sociological factors.

AO3 – This gains up to **2** analysis marks in the final paragraph by stating that behaviours are more homogenised and by evaluating that defining and distinguishing social class is becoming more difficult.

2 3 **8–10** Answers in this band will show good knowledge and understanding of relevant material on two reasons for the difficulty in measuring social mobility.

There will be two developed applications of material from the item, for example how the pay of a job does not necessarily reflect its class, and how social class is defined beyond just employment.

There will be appropriate analysis/evaluation of two reasons, for example analysing the different ways in which a class can be defined beyond occupation and the difficulty of measuring mobility.

4–7 Answers in this band will show limited knowledge and understanding of one or two examples of the difficulty in measuring social mobility.

There will be some successful application of material from the item, for example expanding on why defining class has become difficult in post-modern society.

There will be some analysis/evaluation.

1–3 Answers in this band will show limited knowledge and understanding of measuring social mobility and social class.

There will be limited application of material from the item. Some material may be at a tangent to the question, for example some general discussion about social class unlinked to the question.

There will be little or no analysis/evaluation.

0 No relevant points.

Indicative content

Answers may include the following and/or relevant points.

- Discrepancy between pay and job.
- That class is measured beyond employment.
- Does not consider inheritance or financial windfalls (such as lottery wins).
- Occupations now are often temporary, bonus-related, short-term, thus difficult to measure.
- Defining mobility is difficult, for example absolute/relative mobility.
- Difficult to measure if achievement is ascribed or achieved.

Top band answer

Maximum mark out of 10

3 marks for AO1: Knowledge and understanding

4 marks for AO2: Interpretation and application

3 marks for AO3: Analysis and evaluation

Social mobility refers to the movement between social class hierarchies. Social mobility usually refers to the progression of the working classes up into the middle class. Social class structures and definitions are constantly changing however, and so, as suggested in Item A, it is becoming increasingly difficult to measure the true level of the extent of social mobility.

The first reason for this difficulty in measurement is because social class levels have become increasingly fragmented and it is no longer possible to talk about a simple two- or three-tier class system. Goldthorpe notes that there is a growing middle class but this can then be subdivided into an upper-middle, middle-middle and lower-middle class. Likewise, the working class must also be made distinct from the underclass. The latter is a group that are welfare dependent and therefore cannot be categorised with the working class group. Pakulski and Waters go as far as saying it is near impossible to judge social mobility because social class definitions are dead. This, however, is heavily criticised by many neo-Marxists who believe that social class is still hugely apparent.

A second difficulty in measuring social mobility is because of the ever-changing nature of work, work patterns and income. Due to automation, there has been a huge shift from manual work to the service industries, many businesses have become fragmented or outsource their work, more people work from home and as a result of second-wave feminism there has been a huge increase in female employment. Therefore the nature of work has changed so much that it is almost impossible to measure social mobility today compared to 50 years ago when there was a much clearer distinction between non-manual and manual occupations.

Despite this however, some sociologists believe that it should be easier now to measure social mobility because the gap between the rich and the poor has widened. Westergaard states that social class is becoming more significant than ever before with a clearer distinction between the elite minority and the majority. Therefore measuring social mobility between these two groups should be easier as the true elite is limited to the 1% of super-rich.

Marker's comments

AO1 – This gains up to **3** knowledge and understanding marks by showing a good understanding of social mobility starting with a definition. There is strong knowledge of fragmentation and the changing nature of work as well as key terms such as automation, welfare dependency and privatisation, backed up by sociologists.

AO2 – The answer gains up to **4** marks as it shows a clear interpretation of the question and applies two strong reasons each backed up with a different theory. Point one uses Goldthorpe and Pakulski and Waters as evidence; the second point applies ideas from the feminist perspective. The item is also applied in the introductory paragraph.

AO3 – This gains up to **3** analysis marks by contrasting two very different reasons for the difficulty in measuring social mobility. The concluding paragraph also gains marks by stating a counterargument that class movement should be easier to measure and an evaluation mark is gained for Westergaard's theory.

2 4 **17–20** Answers in this band will show sound, conceptually-detailed knowledge of a range of relevant material on the disadvantages faced in society by ethnic minorities. A sophisticated understanding of the question and of the presented material will be shown.

Appropriate material will be applied accurately and with sensitivity to the issues raised by the question.

Analysis and evaluation will be explicit and relevant. Evaluation may be developed, for instance by contrasting functionalist, Marxist, Weberian and New Right theories. Analysis will show clear explanation and draw appropriate and relevant conclusions.

13–16 Answers in this band will show accurate, broad and/or deep but incomplete knowledge. Understanding of a number of significant aspects of the question; reasonable understanding of the presented material.

Application of the material is largely explicitly relevant to the question, though some material may be inadequately focused.

Some limited explicit evaluation, for example outlining the move towards more equality in post-modern society.

9–12 Answers in this band will show a largely accurate knowledge but limited range and depth, for example a basic account of ethnicity and disadvantage. Understanding will be shown of some aspects of the question; superficial understanding shown of the presented material.

Applying listed material from the general topic area but with limited regard for its relevance to the issues raised by the question, or applying a narrow range of more relevant material.

Evaluation will take the form of a comparison of competing positions or one or two isolated points about ethnicity. Analysis will be limited, with answers tending towards the descriptive.

5–8 Answers in this band will show limited undeveloped knowledge, for example two to three insubstantial points about ethnicity or inequality in general. Understanding of only very limited aspects of the question; simplistic understanding of the presented material.

Limited application of suitable material, and/or material often at a tangent to the demands of the question.

Very limited or no evaluation. Attempts at analysis, if any, are thin and disjointed.

1–4 Answers in this band will show a very limited knowledge, for example one to two very basic points about ethnicity. Very little or no understanding of the question and of the presented material.

Significant errors, omissions, and/or incoherence in application of material.

No analysis or evaluation.

0 No relevant points.

Indicative content

Concepts and issues such as: discrimination in employment, education and policing (examples such as Gifford or Macpherson report may be used); stereotyping; labelling; ethnocentrism; poverty and social class; underclass (linked to Marxism); labour markets (Weberian theory); marginalisation; cultures of resistance; institutionalised/covert/overt racism; unskilled labour; Rex and Tomlinson, Miles, Modood. Counterarguments can focus on functionalist ideas of meritocracy and post-modern theories of globalisation and multiculturalism.

Top band answer

Maximum mark out of 20

8 marks for AO1: Knowledge and understanding

6 marks for AO2: Interpretation and application

6 marks for AO3: Analysis and evaluation

Ethnic minority refers to a group within a community that has different national or cultural traditions from the main population and is often linked to race. Many countries are becoming increasingly multicultural in terms of their ethnic make-up but evidence shows that the minority groups are still likely to be disadvantaged. However, there is also plenty of evidence to suggest that this is changing.

The first evidence of disadvantage as stated in Item B can be seen in terms of employment. Around 14% of the UK population belong to an ethnic minority group but writers such as Rex and Tomlinson show that these groups are still more likely to be at the bottom of the income scale. Bangladeshis and Pakistanis, for example, have the highest unemployment rates in the UK and along with black Caribbeans are the least likely groups to appear in the highest socio-economic group.

This poor distribution of wealth then transmits into housing and living conditions which are likely to be at a much lower standard for ethnic minorities than other groups. The Marxist writer Castle suggests that this ethnic divide of wealth benefits capitalism as this group is more likely to pick up the lower-status jobs and therefore act as a cheap reserve army of labour to fuel the interests of the powerful majority. However, this can be counterargued by the increase in multicultural societies, particularly in the post-modern period.

The Weberian writers Rex and Tomlinson suggest that this causes many ethnic groups to become marginalised from the rest of society into underclass subcultures. These groups then become alienated. There is plenty of evidence of this in regions of London that have become almost exclusively poor Asian areas or black ghettos. This alienation then becomes a self perpetuating continuation through multiple generations.

Further evidence of disadvantage for ethnic minorities can be seen through the attitudes of major institutions such as education and the police force. Writers such as Modood and Gilborn have long provided evidence of an ethnocentric curriculum, meaning that the structure and teaching of education largely ignores the representations of those from ethnic minorities. Subjects such as English Literature and History are often seen to be written from the point of view of the white majority. Despite this, there are many initiatives to create a less ethnocentric curriculum that have taken place in recent times as well as a drive to encourage more black/minority ethnicity (BME) officers into the police force.

In terms of the police force, the Crime Survey for England and Wales shows that ethnic minorities are more likely to be arrested, imprisoned and themselves be the victims of crime. High profile case studies such as the Stephen Lawrence incident have highlighted that there is a serious issue with institutional racism within the police force and Reiner's study identified what he called a canteen culture whereby many police officers harbour stereotypical attitudes towards those from ethnic minorities.

Therefore the statistics speak for themselves: there is no doubt that ethnic minorities are far more likely to suffer disadvantage in countries such as the UK and the USA. However, attitudes, laws and policies regarding race and ethnicity have changed dramatically in the post-modern era and as stated in Item B, it is felt by many that this disadvantage is decreasing all the time.

Pilkington notes that many ethnic minorities do have high social status jobs and actually the labour market position of all ethnic minorities has improved at a faster rate than for white groups. He also notes that many of the disadvantages faced by groups such as Bangladeshis are cultural, such as attitudes to women or language, rather than racist values of others towards that group.

Functionalists also believe that these disadvantages are only temporary until full assimilation has taken place. This means that once an ethnic group becomes fully immersed and integrated into a society then it no longer faces discrimination. Patterson backs up this viewpoint by stating that it is only a matter of time before these issues melt away and that success will be measured on merit rather than ethnic background.

Likewise, post-modernists such as Bauman believe that as a society becomes more multicultural, global and secular then issues surrounding ethnicity become less important. There are now more and more mixed race relationships and children, increased social mobility and far more hybrid identities whereby people mix different cultures together rather than simply sticking to their own indigenous culture.

Controversially, New Right theorists state that many of the disadvantages faced by ethnic minorities are as a result of themselves rather than society. Murray for example states that societies are meritocratic and therefore anyone can succeed if they apply themselves; he believes that many groups blame society and racism rather than admit the issue is with their own unwillingness to push themselves. Marxists disagree with this claim by stating that meritocracy is purely a myth.

Saunders supports this idea as he says that many of the issues ethnic minorities face are because of their unstable single-parent families and dependency on state welfare. It is these factors that cause the groups to fall into underclass deprivation and blaming society masks the real issue of personal blame.

In conclusion, the statistics clearly show that ethnic minorities do face disadvantages compared to others in society, especially in areas such as education and employment, but it must be noted that the discrimination these groups face is nowhere near as harsh as in the past. Attitudes towards racism and ethnic inequality have improved dramatically and this is reflected in a change of laws and policies across many issues.

Although it would be wrong to state that racism and racial inequality have come to an end, there is certainly significant evidence of a less ethnocentric curriculum in education, increased regulation in employment law and closer monitoring of the police. All of these factors combined mean that ethnic minorities face less discrimination and disadvantage than they would have 30 years ago.

Marker's comments

AO1 – This essay gains up to **8** knowledge and understanding marks as it demonstrates a very strong understanding of ethnicity and discrimination including clear definitions in the introduction and a recent census statistic. The essay has good knowledge of theory such as functionalism, post-modernism, New Right and Weberian theory. Understanding is also shown through the variety of key terms such as marginalisation, underclass, subcultures, institutionalised racism and ethnocentrism.

AO2 – Up to **6** marks are gained for interpretation and application which build on the evidence in the item at two points in the essay. The material, theories and evidence to support the arguments can be seen through the application of Castle, Rex, Tomlinson, Modood, Gilborn, Reiner, Pilkington, Bauman and Saunders to support the two lines of argument for and against the statement. Interpretation marks are also awarded for referring to a range of sociological theory but also reference to different ethnic groups. Often essays of this nature only focus on black groups.

AO3 – This essay gains up to **6** analysis marks by clearly contrasting a range of different discriminations in overt, covert and institutionalised forms. Analysis marks are also gained by comparing a range of different sociological perspectives from both left- and right-wing thinking. There are also evaluative marks in the penultimate paragraph gained by discussing policy changes and in the final paragraph by emphasising examples of increased equality.

Paper 3

0 1 **Two marks** for each of **two** appropriate factors clearly outlined or **one mark** for appropriate factors partially outlined, such as those outlined below.

- Government **[1 mark]** have the ability to enforce laws and policies on people **[+1 mark]**.
- Police **[1 mark]** have the right to arrest, fine or give warnings **[+1 mark]**.

- Jail/prison **[1 mark]** – a formal punishment enforced by security/guards **[+1 mark]**.
- Judiciary **[1 mark]** have the power to decide punishments **[+1 mark]**.
- Armed forces **[1 mark]** have power to enforce control and instructions **[+1 mark]**.

Other relevant material should be credited.

No marks for **no** relevant points.

0 2 **Two marks** for each of **three** appropriate reasons clearly outlined or **one mark** for appropriate reasons partially outlined, such as those outlined below.

- Material deprivation **[1 mark]** – often ethnic minority groups live in poorer areas **[+1 mark]**.
- Social/cultural deprivation **[1 mark]** – less conformist behaviours/lack of contacts in society to progress **[+1 mark]**.
- Media representation **[1 mark]** – may be negative or glamorises criminality **[+1 mark]**.
- Negative labelling/targeting **[1 mark]** – more likely to be negatively labelled leading to a self-fulfilling prophecy **[+1 mark]**.
- Police/institutional racism **[1 mark]** – targeted by police or attitude of police force towards ethnic minorities **[+1 mark]**.
- Culture of resistance/marginalisation **[1 mark]** – many groups are pushed to the edges or not accepted in society **[+1 mark]**.

Other relevant material should be credited.

No marks for **no** relevant points.

0 3 **8–10** Answers in this band will show good knowledge and understanding of relevant material on two reasons why white-collar crime is not punished to the same degree as other crimes.

There will be two developed applications of material from the item, for example Marxist views on corruption and inequality, difficulty in detection of white-collar crime, interactionist views on labelling, inequality of government or penal system.

There will be appropriate analysis/evaluation, for example noting that many high-profile cases do come under scrutiny and receive punishment or that attitudes to white-collar crime are changing.

4–7 Answers in this band will show a basic to reasonable knowledge and understanding of one or two reasons why white-collar crime receives less punishment.

There will be some successful application of material from the item, for example expanding on the idea that white-collar crime is difficult to detect or for the police to monitor.

There will be some analysis/evaluation.

1–3 Answers in this band will show limited knowledge and understanding of reasons why white-collar crime in under-punished.

There will be limited or no application of material from the item. Some material may be at a tangent to the question, for example there may be some drift into a general discussion as to what white-collar crime is or examples of white-collar crimes.

There will be little or no analysis/evaluation.

0 No relevant points.

Indicative content

Answers may include the following and/or relevant points:

- Linking Marxism to the ideas of capitalism and greed.

- Marxism and inequality, those in power targeting the lower classes.

- Theorists such as Chambliss/Snider referring to how laws are made to benefit ruling class.

- Interactionist ideas on labelling the working classes as criminals.

- Left realism – ideas on social inequality and policy.

Top band answer

Maximum mark out of 10

3 marks for AO1: Knowledge and understanding

4 marks for AO2: Interpretation and application

3 marks for AO3: Analysis and evaluation

Sutherland defines white-collar crime as a crime committed by a person of respectability and high social status in the course of their occupation. Examples include fraud, forgery or tax evasion. As mentioned in Item A, these crimes often receive far less of a punishment than blue-collar crimes.

According to Marxist sociologists, one reason for the lower punishment of white-collar crimes is due to the corruption and inequality in the structure of society. Althusser suggests that the superstructure of society is ruled by the bourgeoisie and so the government, police force and law systems are all controlled by the rich. This means that they are more likely to evade punishment as they are the group controlling society, an example being false expenses claims made by politicians that went largely unpunished. Althusser refers to this as the ideological state apparatus. These ideas are often viewed as outdated, however, as issues such as tax evasion have recently become big news.

A second reason is due to social capital and labelling. Bourdieu notes that even if a white-collar criminal is caught they can use the system of the old boys' network to reduce or eradicate the penalty. This often means that the criminal has contacts in the government, police force or can afford the very best legal aid. This in turn relates to the interactionist's labelling theory in that those who are negatively labelled as criminals and become the scapegoats are the proletariat while the bourgeoisie escape detection and punishment. However, it is often suggested that it is now more difficult to judge the social class of a person, especially with an expanding middle class.

Despite these views, however, it must be noted that increasingly white-collar crimes are being pursued and targeted because of public concern, anger and outrage. For example, the police now monitor the use of illegal offshore bank accounts far more rigorously than they did in the past.

Marker's comments

AO1 – This gains up to **3** knowledge and understanding marks by outlining a clear definition of white-collar crime in the introduction and providing examples. There is also a clear understanding of two reasons for low punishment in terms of corruption and the old boys' network; this is also linked to Marxist and interactionist theory.

AO2 – The answer gains up to **4** marks as it shows a clear interpretation of the question and applies the item. There is a clear interpretation of two very strong reasons for the lower punishment of white-collar crime and each one applies a theorist in the form of Althusser then Bourdieu. Each of these paragraphs contains two strong AO2 marks.

AO3 – This gains up to **3** analysis marks by linking and analysing white-collar crime from a Marxist and interactionist perspective. Evaluation marks are gained at the end of the paragraphs and in the concluding paragraph which suggests a counterargument to the statement that white-collar crime is always less punished.

0 4 **25–30** Answers in this band will show sound, conceptually detailed knowledge of a range of relevant material of interactionist approaches to crime. Sophisticated understanding of the question will be shown, and of the presented material.

Appropriate material will be applied accurately and with sensitivity to the issues raised by the question.

Analysis and evaluation will be explicit and relevant. Evaluation may be developed for example by using alternative perspectives (such as functionalism and Marxism) to criticise the approach taken by interactionists.

Analysis will show clear explanation. Appropriate conclusions will be drawn.

19–24 Answers in this band will show accurate, broad and/or deep but incomplete knowledge. Understanding of a number of significant aspects of the question will be shown, along with good understanding of the presented material.

Application of the material is largely explicitly relevant to the question, though some material may be inadequately focused.

Some limited explicit evaluation, for example evaluating the labelling theory and/or some appropriate analysis of the interactionist ideas of primary and secondary deviance.

13–18 Answers in this band will show a largely accurate knowledge but limited range and depth, for example a broadly accurate, if basic, account of the interactionist view on crime. Understanding of some aspects of the question will be shown along with superficial understanding of the presented material.

Applying listed material from the general topic area but with limited regard for its relevance to the issues raised by the question, or applying a narrow range of more relevant material.

Evaluation will take the form of a comparison of competing positions or one to two isolated stated points. Analysis will be limited, with answers tending towards the descriptive.

7–12 Answers in this band will show limited undeveloped knowledge, for example two to three insubstantial points on interactionist theory in general. Understanding of only very limited aspects of the question will be shown along with simplistic understanding of the presented material.

Limited application of suitable material, and/or material often at a tangent to the demands of the question, for example drifting into a discussion on generic interactionism unlinked to crime or crime in general.

Very limited or no evaluation. Attempts at analysis, if any, are thin and disjointed.

1–6 Answers in this band will show a very limited knowledge, for example one to two very basic points about crime and deviance in general. Very little or no understanding of the question and of the presented material is shown.

Significant errors, omissions, and/or incoherence in application of material.

No analysis or evaluation.

0 No relevant points.

Indicative content

Concepts and issues such as the following may appear: labelling and self-fulfilling prophecy; deviancy reaction (Becker); Young and marijuana users; primary and secondary deviance (Lemert); looking glass self; I and the Me and master status. Counterarguments can look at issues from other perspectives as well as Akers, Taylor, Walton and Young, Gouldner, Cicourel and Braithwaite, etc.

Top band answer

Maximum mark out of 30

12 marks for AO1: Knowledge and understanding

9 marks for AO2: Interpretation and application

9 marks for AO3: Analysis and evaluation

Interactionist sociologists are interpretivists, which means that they look at the subject of crime from the point of view of the individual, conducting micro research in an attempt to understand the reasons behind offences. However, interactionist research has been criticised, especially from positivist researchers.

As noted in Item B, interpretivists focus on the idea that it is often the act that is labelled as deviant or criminal as opposed to the individual themselves. Becker noted that the same behaviour can gain different reactions dependent on the social situation. He uses the example of nudity as evidence for this in that it would be classed as a social norm in your home but as deviant or even criminal if conducted in a public place.

Becker notes that it is the reaction of others that makes the individual recognise what is deviant. This theory demonstrates then that deviance does not only change from society to society but also over time; therefore Becker concludes that crime and deviance are simply social constructions. However, many would say that certain crimes are deviant prior to their labelling and the offenders are well aware of their actions prior to the public reaction.

This idea is further backed up by the work of Lemert who refers to primary and secondary deviance. Primary deviance is the initial deviant act itself. The more important part, however, is secondary deviance which is when the individual commits further acts having accepted their label as a deviant or a criminal. For example, once a burglar has accepted their label, they will carry out the act on a more frequent basis.

Lemert's theory relates to the self-fulfilling prophecy principle in that often the individual will feel the weight of the label on their shoulders and begin to self-perpetuate the expectations society has dictated for them. This may explain why so many criminals and ex-prisoners go on to re-offend through their lives. This, however, does not take into account those that are fully rehabilitated or break the negative labels that are attached to them.

Goffman further demonstrates this idea in his study on mental illness: he found that the negative label of being referred to as 'mad' causes the patients to not only conform to this label but in many cases increase their anti-social behaviour. Goffman referred to this type of identity as a master status; a label which supersedes all other identities.

A final example to show the effects of labelling can be seen in Jock Young's classic study of marijuana users in Notting Hill. Once labelled as a hippy or a druggy, this became the user's main identity or master status. The negative response of those around them and the police simply made the drug use more significant in their lives and simply served to enhance their overall drug usage. Young's study has of course received criticism for failing to acknowledge those that used the drug sporadically without falling into the master status identification.

For interactionists then, the importance of defining crime and deviance can only be understood when applied to the individual's situation and also considering the reaction to others. However, other sociologists disagree and believe that an act can be criminal or deviant on a universal level without the interpretation of others.

Taylor, Walton and Young, for example, note that many individuals know that the act they are committing is deviant before they carry out the act but it is they themselves that make the decision to still do it or not. Taking Becker's theory of nudity as an example, a youth that decides to streak at a sporting event is well aware of the reaction they will get before they conduct the act.

Akers continues this debate by arguing that individuals are not powerless in shaping their own identities but rather it is a choice that individuals make in shaping their personality. He believes it is rather naïve to suggest that a criminal is unaware that what they do is wrong or that they will not get a reaction; it is a personal choice they have pre-determined.

Indeed, many post-modernist theorists such as Lyotard believe that it is becoming more evident that individuals may purposely choose deviant behaviour in an attempt to shape a social identity in an increasingly homogeneous society whereby competition for uniqueness is difficult. Foucault refers to this as the process of individualism. This contrasts to the interactionist perspective that it is others that bestow the label onto the offender.

Perhaps the biggest criticism of interactionist theory however comes from the Marxist perspective. They believe that interpretivists ignore the role of power in understanding crime and deviance. Box notes that certain groups have the power to influence what is classified as criminal or socially acceptable. In other words there is one law for the rich and another for the poor. A person of lower social status is far more likely to be seen as a criminal compared to a person of high social status even if the act committed was exactly the same.

Taylor, Walton and Young go on to say that crime is not a result of others' labelling but rather as a direct result of capitalism as it is a competitive system that encourages aggression and a determination to earn more money and a higher status than your fellow man. It is a system of exploitation at the expense of others and thus encourages criminal behaviour.

Therefore, the interactionist viewpoint is an interesting one and it helps us to understand the activity of deviance from an individual point of view and enables us to consider the reactions of others. However, the theory does not really take into account the structure of society in order to understand behaviour.

To truly understand levels of crime and deviance in a society you need to look at the economic structure, the political system and the environment first before you begin to analyse the behaviour of people on an individual level. A combination of these factors will lead researchers to a better understanding of deviant behaviour.

Marker's comments

AO1 – This essay gains up to **12** knowledge and understanding marks as it demonstrates a very strong grasp of the interactionist view on crime. The essay begins with a definition of interactionism and describes the theory accurately before also showing understanding of post-modernism and Marxism. There is liberal use of key terms such as labelling, self-fulfilling prophecy, primary and secondary deviance and master status for the interpretivist approach and homogenisation and capitalism in the counterarguments. All the content and concepts are relevant to the question.

AO2 – Up to **9** marks are gained here as there is clear interpretation of the question and this can be seen through the use and development of the item as well as key concepts, studies and theories throughout the essay. There is application of a range of interactionist writers such as Becker, Lemert, Goffman and Young. In counterargument there is application of classic studies such as Taylor, Walton and Young but also Akers and Lyotard from the post-modern approach. All of these studies support arguments for or against the debate.

AO3 – This essay gains **9** analysis marks through outlining the interactionist approach before using critical analysis from the Marxist and post-modern angle. Analysis therefore comes from the contrast of individual behaviours compared to societal factors for crime. Evaluation is evident throughout and emphasised in the final paragraphs which conclude with evidence of how interactionist ideas need to be combined with other approaches in order to offer a more valid picture.

05 **8–10** Answers in this band will show very good knowledge and understanding of two disadvantages of using covert observation in sociological research.

There will be two applications of relevant material for example the lack of informed consent/deception/ unethicality; the danger or risk of being identified.

There will be appropriate analysis, for example why positivists are critical of the observational technique.

4–7 Answers in this band will show a reasonable to good knowledge and understanding of one or two disadvantages of using covert observation in sociological research.

There will be one or two applications of relevant material, for example comparing covert observations to another method with more advantages.

There will be some basic analysis.

1–3 Answers in this band will show limited knowledge and little or no understanding of the question or the material.

There will be limited focus on the question, for example there may be some general description of what covert observations are or a focus on advantages instead.

There will be limited or no analysis.

0 No relevant points.

Indicative content

Answers may include the following and/or other relevant points.

- No informed consent/deception.
- Risk of being identified/putting researcher in dangerous position.
- Difficulty getting in/staying in/getting out.
- Issues of 'going native' with the sample.
- Lack of control, being able to ask probing questions.
- Difficulty in recording material and keeping recording equipment covert.

Top band answer

Maximum mark out of 10

5 marks for AO1: Knowledge and understanding

3 marks for AO2: Interpretation and application

2 marks for AO3: Analysis and evaluation

Covert observation refers to those studies that take place undercover without the knowledge, permission or understanding of the sample group. Covert observations can be conducted in either a participant or non-participant fashion but they do have several disadvantages as a research method.

One criticism of this method is that it often breaks ethical guidelines and practice; it is often referred to as deception to observe the behaviour of an individual or group without their informed consent. One such example is Humphreys' 'tearoom trade' study observing homosexual activity in public places. Humphreys used licence plate numbers to track the sample group. He falsely acted as a 'watch queen' and followed the individuals to their homes. Therefore the study has been heavily criticised for privacy violations and deceit. Indeed, many pieces of research have been discredited by universities because of the unethical nature of using the covert observation technique.

A second criticism of covert observations is the high levels of risk the sociologist puts themselves under, especially when involved in dangerous or illegal activities. In Venkatesh's 'gang leader for a day' study he was actually held captive as a hostage for 24 hours by drug dealers due to their concern as to who this stranger was in their neighbourhood. Venkatesh had put himself at an extreme level of risk. Becoming too involved with the sample group is known as going native. It is often the case that sociologists have found themselves wrapped up in not only precarious situations but often in illegal scenarios too.

Despite these concerns however, covert observations often produce some of the most interesting research findings and in particular are ideal in terms of gaining valid results full of accuracy and detail. Without observing behaviour in a covert manner, research suffers from the Hawthorne effect which is detrimental to understanding human behaviour in its natural form.

Marker's comments

AO1 – This gains up to **5** knowledge and understanding marks by showing a very clear understanding of covert observation throughout. Marks are gained for a clear definition of covert observation in the introduction. Sound knowledge of informed consent and risk are applied as well as terms such as deception, unethical and going native used within the essay. There is also strong knowledge of studies to back up the two arguments.

AO2 – The answer gains up to **3** marks as it shows a clear interpretation of the question and applies relevant theorists in the form of Humphreys and Venkatesh. There is also good interpretation of the question by using a classic study and a more contemporary piece of research. There are also two very clear reasons applied, backed up with evidence.

AO3 – This gains up to **2** analysis marks in the overall concluding paragraph, making an analysis of how covert observations gain valid information and also evaluating that if the research were overt then it would suffer from the Hawthorne effect.

06 **17–20** Answers in this band will show accurate, conceptually detailed knowledge and sound understanding of a range of relevant material on the usefulness of functionalist theories in our understanding of society. Sophisticated understanding of the question and of the presented material will be shown.

Appropriate material will be applied accurately and with sensitivity to the issues raised by the question.

Analysis and evaluation will be explicit and relevant. Evaluation may be developed for example through a debate between different perspectives, e.g. functionalism, neo-functionalism, Marxism, feminism, interactionism, post-modernism, etc. Analysis will show clear explanation. Appropriate conclusions will be drawn.

13–16 Answers in this band will show accurate, broad and/or deep but incomplete knowledge. Understanding of a number of significant aspects of the question will be shown along with good understanding of the presented material.

Application of material is largely explicitly relevant to the question, though some material may be inadequately focused.

Some limited explicit evaluation, for example from a Marxist perspective, and/or some appropriate analysis, for example clear explanations of some of the presented material.

9–12 Answers in this band will show largely accurate knowledge but limited range and depth, including a broadly accurate, if basic, account of some of the functionalist theory. Understanding of some limited but significant aspects of the question will be shown along with superficial understanding of the presented material.

Applying listed material from the general topic area but with limited regard for its relevance to the issues raised by the question, or applying a narrow range of more relevant material.

Evaluation will take the form of a comparison of competing positions or one to two isolated stated points. Analysis will be limited, with answers tending towards the descriptive.

5–8 Answers in this band will show limited undeveloped knowledge, for example two to three insubstantial points about functionalism. Understanding of only very limited aspects of the question; simplistic understanding of the presented material.

Limited application of suitable material, and/or material often at a tangent to the demands of the question, for example perhaps drifting into an unfocused description of consensus with limited reference to functionalism.

Very limited to no evaluation. Attempts at analysis, if any, are thin and disjointed.

1–4 Answers in this band will show very limited knowledge, for example one to two very insubstantial points about sociological theory in general. Very little/no understanding of the question and the presented material.

Significant errors, omissions, and/or omissions in application of material or some material ineffectually recycled from the item.

No analysis or evaluation.

0 No relevant points.

Indicative content

Concepts and issues such as the following may appear: value consensus; mechanical solidarity; organic analogy/solidarity; functional fit; structuralism; sub-systems; institutions; anomie; social integration; Durkheim, Parsons, Murdock; functional prerequisites; social control; latency; agencies of socialisation; macrosociology; differences between traditional and neo-functionalism and counterarguments with other contrasting perspectives.

Top band answer

Maximum mark out of 20

8 marks for AO1: Knowledge and understanding

6 marks for AO2: Interpretation and application

6 marks for AO3: Analysis and evaluation

Functionalism is a classic theory within sociology and adopts a positivist approach to understanding human behaviour. This means the focus is on social structures and how they shape society.

Functionalists tend to look at the positive aspects of society but as mentioned in Item C, they have been criticised for ignoring the abundance of negative issues that exist within all societies around the world.

Early writers such as Comte and later Durkheim looked at the idea of consensus. That is, the idea that society needs to be understood by looking at the correlations and relationships between various institutions and how these act as the glue for holding society together. Durkheim believed that strong moral entities such as family, education and religion could drive order and solidarity in a society resulting in what he called 'value consensus'.

This view is further backed up by the organic analogy theory by Parsons. He believed that the agencies of socialisation such as political, economic and cultural sub-systems act in the same way as the organs of a human body. By this he means that all the institutions are co-dependent on each other in the same way that the parts of a human body work together in order to survive. Parsons argued that these systems working together allow for survival, order, socialisation and social integration.

Murdock continues this argument by using the example of the nuclear family. In order for a family to function there needs to be clearly defined roles: the man takes the instrumental role and the woman takes the expressive role and by working together as a team the family can function as a unit, as each person is working a mechanism to keep the well-oiled family machine working. This theory is of course heavily criticised by liberal feminists who believe that families should be more symmetrical with joint conjugal roles.

Parsons further demonstrates the effects of this model of human behaviour through the 'functional fit' theory. This identified that humans adapt as society changes such as through pre-industrial, post-industrial, urbanisation and into modern industrial society. Neo-functionalist Avis refers to this as the organisation of human capital, that humans will adapt to structural and economic changes in society in order to maintain essential consensus and social stability.

However, despite being one of the classic studies in sociology, functionalism has been heavily criticised for being an outdated theory and, as mentioned in Item C, for only focusing on how society works rather than looking at where society can break down and become dysfunctional. Indeed, Merton has identified several issues within the model of functionalism.

Arguably the strongest critiques of functionalism come from the Marxist perspective. Marxists believe that functionalists place too much emphasis on looking at consensus in society and in doing so ignore issues of conflict. In particular Marxists believe that functionalists ignore the dissatisfaction people have in society due to the unfair distribution of wealth under capitalism. Marx and Engels argued that you cannot have a system of solidarity when there is a direct conflict of interest between the bourgeoisie and the proletariat.

Althusser states that societies are not based on consensus but rather they are structured to benefit the ruling classes. He refers to this as the state apparatus. He identifies the government, education system and legal systems as maintaining stability but only by the powerful enforcing their rules and regulations on to a submissive and oppressed group at the bottom of society. For Althusser, functionalism fails to recognise how society is run on the exploitation of the proletariat by being forced to accept an oppressive superstructure and not through the willingness of people.

Likewise, feminist theorists also believe that functionalism ignores conflict in society; in particular they state that attention is not paid to the issue of patriarchy. For example, Murdock stated how the family works with defined roles. However writers such as Oakley and Dworkin say that this family unit is only functioning at the expense and exploitation of the woman. The woman is expected to carry out key tasks in the family without benefiting from the financial gain or authority that the man gains.

Finally, interactionist sociologists such as Mead and Cooley criticise functionalism for dedicating too much focus towards societal factors rather that individuality. Interactionists believe that much of human behaviour is driven by the individual and personal choice rather than being shaped by society. In fact Mead says that humans present a false persona in society compared to how they actually feel on the inside, a concept he referred to as the 'I and the Me'. Therefore the social action approach to sociology sees functionalism as both outdated and limited.

Therefore, although functionalist theory is very interesting to study as a historical understanding of sociology, it does seem rather outdated in contemporary society. For example the importance of religion is overstated compared to the more secular society we have today. Post-modernists such as Baudrillard and Lyotard, for example, point to factors such as globalisation and multiculturalism as defining features in many societies which contrast massively to the world that Durkheim was writing about.

Perhaps functionalism is still relevant to developing countries based on traditional roles and the importance of religion but for many increasingly secular western societies, functionalist theory has become rather antiquated and redundant.

Marker's comments

AO1 – This essay gains up to **8** knowledge and understanding marks as it demonstrates a very strong understanding of functionalist theory throughout. There is a clear explanation in the introduction of what functionalism is. Understanding is demonstrated through ideas such as value consensus, organic analogy, agencies of socialisation, instrumental and expressive roles and the functional fit theory. Functionalism is also contrasted with ideas from feminism, Marxism and interactionist perspectives.

AO2 – **6** marks are gained for interpretation and application through first using and building on the item. There is application of writers such as Comte, Durkheim, Parsons, Murdock and neo-functionalist Avis in the arguments for the item. In the counterarguments there is application of studies from the likes of Althusser, Oakley, Dworkin, Mead and Cooley. There is strong interpretation of the question here by understanding the time at which functionalist theory was written.

AO3 – This essay gains **6** analysis marks through having an equal balance outlining functionalist theory and then using other perspectives as a critical analysis. There is also analysis between traditional classic studies in sociology contrasted to more contemporary research. There is a strong concluding paragraph that evaluates functionalism through the use of the post-modern perspective.